Acorns Among the Grass

Adventures in Eco-therapy

T0306838

Acorns Among the Grass

Adventures in Eco-therapy

Caroline Brazier

BOOKS

Winchester, UK
Washington, USA

First published by O-Books, 2011
O-Books is an imprint of John Hunt Publishing Ltd., Laurel House, Station Approach,
Alresford, Hants, SO24 9JH, UK
office1@o-books.net
www.o-books.com

For distributor details and how to order please visit the 'Ordering' section on our website.

Text copyright: Caroline Brazier 2010

ISBN: 978 1 84694 619 6

A CIP catalogue record for this book is available from the British Library.

Design: Stuart Davies

Printed in the UK by CPI Antony Rowe
Printed in the USA by Offset Paperback Mfrs, Inc

We operate a distinctive and ethical publishing philosophy in all
areas of our business, from our global network of authors to
production and worldwide distribution.

CONTENTS

Previous books by author

Buddhist Psychology (2003) Constable Robinson
The Other Buddhism (2007) O-Books
Guilt: an exploration (2009) O-Books
Listening to the Other (2009) O-Books
Other-Centred Therapy (2009) O-Books

Prologue

Summer 2010 we advertise a week of eco-therapy to be run at the Amida retreat centre which is situated in a forgotten corner of rural France. We, in this instance, are a small Buddhist community, whose main base is in Narborough, a small village just outside Leicester. Our French house is in the ancient region of Berry, right in the middle of France. Thus we travel between bases in the centres of two countries, central England and central France. We centre ourselves and our practice.

In England, we, that being the Amida community, run training programmes in Buddhist approaches to psychotherapy. We refer to our work as Other-Centred Approach. Ours is a well established programme, having run in this form for more than fifteen years, and a further fifteen before that without its Buddhist underpinnings overtly displayed. I often teach with David, my former husband, but this eco-therapy week I am working with Sundari. She and I have run weekends on environmental themes before back in England, but we have never previously had a clear week in which to explore the work together. This is thus a new experience of working together. The expanse of time and space (five working days and thirty acres of land; woodland and rough fields, long abandoned by the large white charolais cattle who once grazed them) create a canvass on which we work a tapestry of activities.

Our group assembles. We are joined by regular members of our community, people who know the terrain and who themselves run sessions from time to time: Massimo, who runs bio-dance workshops; Sumaya, who has been leading the community out in France through the spring; Susthama, who supports so much of the work which I do with her practicality and wisdom; Simon, an art therapist and Buddhist trainee; and Kaspa, who works with theatre methods. Others are students or regular participants in our training events. The week unfolds.

Nature is healing. We have always known this. It speaks with myriad voices in the silence of wordlessness, whispering comfort and wisdom.

For me this is not just a training event, but a marker, a point of change, a fulcrum. It is the turning of our working year and the end of a period of time in which I have experienced substantial changes in my personal life. Several others too are in the midst of questions, searching for meaning and facing difficult life choices. Together we are journeying; new tracks, wilderness crossings. Through attention and conversation with the elements around us, we explore and discover the freedom to change. We learn once more to wonder.

When the eco-therapy week is over, I start to write. Images and ideas crowd my head and the muse chases me into places of reflection. This book is the result. An account of a group and of a summer, interwoven with the ideas and therapeutic theory which framed our work, it is an invitation to share, to join the exploration and to experience the process of engagement in a healing relationship with nature.

Some passages in it are descriptive, drawing me back into the immediacy of the surroundings as I write. Others are analytical, discursive, drawing theory from the practical experiences. As such, the book is both specific and universal, a dance of scenes and activities, commonplace enough to be familiar to anyone who has wandered off the concrete pavements of the city into the wilder places of our planet, yet unique to a moment and a place. Most of the content belongs to this summer, a few weeks of living close to the earth, but some of my accounts hark back to earlier experiences. All are first hand, concrete and reflective.

The year circles on. The group dispersed, carrying impressions of grasses and trees, becomes a memory. Brambles grow across the paths, recently trodden. When we return, we cut their searching tendrils back. Next summer we will need new paths.

But still in the field where we danced last summer, acorns lie beneath the old oak trees among the grass of the field, waiting for springtime.

Chapter One

The Earth Element

We stand in a circle on the earth.

We have gathered under the old walnut in front of the house. It is an ancient tree, but there are young branches growing out of the old trunk. They bow down elbow deep into the long grass of the field; sweeping curved twigs, their large oval leaves fluttering on thick green stems, with the nearly formed globes of walnuts swaddled amongst them.

The trunk is hollow, torn off in some long past storm, and edged by jagged bark. Some years ago we had kittens at the house, and they loved to run up inside the belly of the old tree and peer precariously out of the various openings left by broken boughs, small heads, curious and bright eyed, peeping from the old trunk. Still the tree rewards us most years with crops of walnuts. The fresh nuts are wet and convoluted like little brains, coated in soft brown skin within the hard shells. They fall, tumbling out of the splitting husks as we shake the old tree. We search for them with our feet amongst the grass where they lie, hidden from sight, but easy to find when you stand on them.

Today, though, we are touching the earth.

Although we are wearing shoes, our feet are still capable of sensing the undulations of the rough soil. We place them firmly on the ground, noticing the clumps of field grass, knobbly and uneven beneath them. We close our eyes to feel the unevenness more intensely. We are not used to sensing with our feet.

Modern floors and pavements have made us lazy. We walk along deep in conversation, or preoccupied with day to day thoughts of tasks and fears and loves and lists. We place our feet on an assumption of an even surface and are affronted by objects which interrupt our thoughts. We mutter and grumble as we trip on broken paving stones or falter on uneven floorboards, or stub our toes on unexpected kerbs or tree roots.

Our footwear limits our experience of walking on the earth. We totter on stiletto heels or skid on glass-smooth leather soles. We lace ourselves into sturdy walking boots, sometimes, but not always, with good reason. We dull the sensation in our feet with thick socks or tight stockings.

We limit ourselves to familiar safe places when we walk, taking marked paths and routes we know well. Even in country parks we are choosy about our contact with the ground. Chicken wire and boards cover the boggy places and shredded bark pathways absorb the mud so that we do not trample it home, or into the visitors' centre. We are protected so that we can visit wilder spaces safely and comfortably.

But here we do not need protection. We give attention to the earth. We feel the ground and, in feeling it, ourselves become grounded.

Our feet make an imprint in whatever we stand on, and we feel for that shape as it accommodates to our shoes, which in turn make contact with the soil. Be specific. Observe with care. Investigate. Feeling our way into the body sense is not always easy. For many people the foot is cut off from awareness. Not experienced as a sensing part of the body, the feet are simply treated as functional appendages, not really inhabited, but distanced. Here, in this, our first exercise of the day, we seek to develop our capacity for sensation, allowing our feet-sense to open up, inviting the thousands of nerve-endings which are encompassed in these sense organs to experience the earth.

How does your weight distribute? Do you stand on your heels or your toes? Do your insteps touch your shoes or stand proud? If you shift your weight gently, slightly, backward and forward, do you feel the scrunch of grass stubble beneath your shoes or the knottiness of a twig?

Our bodies function perfectly well without our conscious control. We do not need to know how they enable us to stand, and yet in noticing this, we can wonder at their capacities. We feel our feet working. They work automatically, without needing us to instruct them. They adapt. They hold us upright, cementing us to the earth and yet supporting our posture so that we can stand tall above it. A complex mechanism of bones and sinews, cartilage and muscle, encased in skin, they adjust and tune their structure to the purpose for which the processes of evolution have constructed them.

We breathe deep, the flow of oxygen flooding into our circulation, chasing round through our arteries and veins, down into that place of contact with the ground. The soles of our feet are nourished, just as every other cell in our bodies is, by the breath, the oxygen, the blood. They are living, breathing tissue.

Just as the tree is rooted in the soil, so too, we imagine extending our consciousness down into the ground on which we stand. The walnut tree roots find their way through cracks in the limestone beneath the sparse soil of the field, down into the pockets of clay between the sheets of rock, down into the clefts and crannies where nutrient rich water soaks between the particles of soil. They seek out the water table, hidden from the parched grass of the summer hayfield, but still available to the deep rooted species of plants. Life relies upon such hidden resources. Growth draws on its presence. We feel our own rootedness in the earth and our bodies' connection to the elements of which they are composed. We sense experientially the inseparability for our feet and the ground.

As humans we cannot fly. Our bodies, heavy with flesh, are of the earth. We always rest upon the ground; some ground, some way. Not always conscious of that connection, mediated by buildings or clothing, or mindlessness, we may be separated in awareness from this basal truth; but yet the gravity of our lives is built on foundations of earth from birth to death. And in that death to the earth we return; earth to earth, ashes to ashes and dust to dust. So we sense our earth-ness and in our sensing we are drawn back to the source.

The earth is our mother. Mythologies have wrapped their veils of colour around this truth. Science has bared its veracity to the bone. Both have told us what we already know, deep in our being, for we are earthlings, weaving our lives upon the thin layer of life that clothes our green-blue planet, spinning here within the ocean of space. And in her warm fleshed bosom we plant our feet. We walk, we touch, we embrace her surface.

Elementally we are the same. Solid boned, composed of matter, carbon, calcium, iron, we incorporate the substances, the minerals, mined from deep in the planet's womb by natural processes of water, fire and decomposition; substances that become the building blocks of life. We draw from the earth our life blood, and in its magnetic propensity align maybe with terrestrial fields. As migrating birds, we sense perhaps our orientation to the land and in doing so find direction.

And so we stand, together, each feeling uniquely our relationship to the universal, sharing in the commonality of the circle, joining in exploration of our wider connections with the natural processes.

Working with the environment, we begin with the earth. How could it be otherwise? The experience of simply walking, touching the earth, is the foundation for all other work. It is so basic that we might easily ignore the need to focus our attention upon it in our impatience to engage with other aspects of nature, and yet to avoid such contact misses the opportunity to ground our work. Without it, we float into activities still caught in the mind's morass. Rather, there is a need now to focus, to descend into our roots and to contact our body-sense as it rests in its natural abode, in relationship to the earth.

Other-centred work is about relationship. In this model of

working we connect with and investigate what is true. We allow the world to speak to us, to embrace us and to educate us. We listen to the other, and appreciate the other's mystery. We notice the way our minds harness the other to our own ends, subverting experience to reinforce our stories about the world. We see the constant striving of the mind, the self, to control what cannot be controlled. We understand the fear and grief that drive these processes. As such, this other-centred approach, though used in many ways to explore many sorts of relating, is suited particularly to working with the environment. For in our most basic nature it is to the earth that we relate.

Our relationship to the earth is one of literal dependence. We depend upon the ground with each step that we take. We walk. Step by step, our feet embrace the solidity of the earth and it receives us. Each time we take a step forwards, our feet leave the ground but always then return to it. There is a parting and a coming back together. Each step we take, we are reminded of the soil to which we are bound in this life; of our origin and our last resting place.

We can practise walking with awareness. We can feel our contact with the floor as it changes its quality within each step. The movement of the foot, the engagement of heel and toe, toe and heel. We can place each step gently, consciously on the earth, sensing the particulars of each place on which it rests, the contours, the resistance. We can feel the soft, springy grass, the prominence of a stump of blackthorn cut close to the ground, the hard surface of stone cobbles or the uneven turf of the field. If we close our eyes or walk in the dark on a moonless night, our feet can sense when we leave the path and accidentally stray onto the rough verge.

This week we are exploring our relationship to the earth. Sundari and I are running a group which focuses on our relationship to the environment as part of the August programme at our retreat centre in France. We begin with a grounding exercise. This is our usual practice during this group, so that as we go forth we walk consciously and silently, using our senses and particularly our feet-sense to tune into the spaces which we walk through. We will look with our feet as well as our eyes and ears.

Breathing aligns with the steps, a gentle flow of air in and out of the body as we walk. It is as if we breathe with our feet. Or perhaps we walk with our lungs. As the breathing relaxes, our bodies relax, and with the relaxation we trust ourselves more deeply to the walking. The shoulders lose their stiffness and the belly releases its tension. The spine is straight and open. We feel the breeze on our faces and the air entering our nostrils. We smile. Our eyes and ears are awake to the sights and sounds that arrive but they are not searching, not compulsive. We simply walk.

Working with the Earth Element

One of the early Buddhist meditations was a meditation on the elements. It seems that the early women disciples of the Buddha in particular used this practice. The meditation consists of taking each of the five elements, earth, air, fire, water and space, in turn, and reflecting on its presence both in the world and in the body. The first of these, the earth element, consists of all the solid matter.

So, in practising this meditation, firstly the nuns reflected on all the solid things which they encountered. The earth element occurred not just in the ground upon which they sat, but also in the stones and wood with which people built their homes, the baked clay bowls which the nuns carried, and all the physical objects which they used in daily life. They would then reflect upon solid objects in the body. Bones, teeth, finger and toe nails, faeces are all bodily manifestations of the earth element.

Through this practice, the nuns explored the physicality of the body and of the world in the same way, distinguishing in each how solid components make up a part of the whole. The intention was to recognise experientially that the body and the world are both composed of the same basic elements.

In sharing this practice we also learn to break down the divide between the body, with which we identify, and the rest of the world. We challenge the separation between what is 'me' and what is 'everything else'. We come to understand our existence as creatures of flesh and bone, physical beings with solid presence. So when we stand on the earth, we recognise that we are of the earth. We are here on this planet as collections of solid matter, assembled according to a blueprint carried in our genetic legacy.

The limestone on which our centre in France is built is made up of the skeletons of millions of creatures which lived and died in an ocean that existed millennia ago. Our own skeletons upon which we rely in order to exist and stand and move are made of calcium derivatives also. As we stand on the earth at the start of our exploration, we stand upon the same material, more or less, as that of which our bones are made.

To explore the natural world is to explore our embodiedness. To explore our embodiedness is to explore the world of nature. Our bodies are made up of elements, physical matter, just as all other living and non-living things upon this planet are. We are not different. We grow and change and have physical needs just as other creatures do. It is through the solidity of our bodies that we connect with others and with the earth.

Travelling light

In our modern world, we protect ourselves in all sorts of ways from the forces of nature.

Many people fear discomfort. As soon as the first drops of rain start to fall, umbrellas appear on the streets. People are anxious that clothes and hairstyles will be ruined, that they will catch colds, or simply that they will get wet and uncomfortable.

Whilst our ancestors lived with damp for much of the year, we avoid it even in small quantities, living in houses built to modern standards with damp courses and insulation. We reassure ourselves that this is necessary for public health, but more than anything, we seek it in order to feel comfortable.

We wear shoes out of doors except in very rare circumstances, such as on the beach or, maybe, daringly, on grassy lawns in summer. We wear slippers in the house, anxious about getting cold feet, despite the fact that we have central heating. We have hiking boots for rough terrain, with ankle support lest we tread awkwardly on uneven ground and injure our joints. We have Wellington boots for wet conditions lest we get muddy. Yet children on the streets of Delhi kick footballs with bare feet. In New Zealand they go barefoot to school all the summer.

We have weatherproof clothes to walk on the moors. Breathable jackets keep us free of damp, both inner and outer, letting perspiration out, and keeping rain out too. We have over-trousers and boots with special soles to cushion our feet, woolly hats and expensive, insulated gloves. Sports often seem to need special clothes too these days. We have lycra cycling leggings and wet suits for swimming in the sea, technological running shoes and fashionable outfits for the gym.

Sunshine is no better. We avoid the sun by putting on broad-brimmed hats and sunglasses and slapping on sunscreen so that we do not burn. Some such protection is of course beneficial, but some simply adds complications to life. We use protective clothes because we are afraid of dangers, but these dangers are often vague and undefined. We think of it as foolhardy to attempt activities without the proper equipment, yet throughout the centuries people have made great treks across continents with little more than the clothes they stood up in and a few provisions packed in bundles or saddle bags.

Whether or not we really need the things we insist on having, the effect of increasing urbanisation and affluence has been to erect barriers between modern people and nature. Going out into the countryside is rarely a matter of simply walking out of doors, but more commonly involves assembling such a collection of specialised equipment that we are weighed down, prevented from really engaging with the places that we visit. Quick to cancel if conditions turn inclement, too often rain stops play and we end up watching the natural world on the television screen from our armchairs instead of actually experiencing it directly.

To really encounter the natural world, we must travel light. This is not to say that we should go out unequipped. Of course, if one is walking deep into the moors or climbing in the mountains, it is foolhardy not to take the necessary gear. We need to protect from the sun and snow, extremes of heat and cold, dehydration and exposure, and other real risks. But travelling light means challenging our assumptions about what is essential. Letting encumbrances go, we become free to experience the natural world as it impacts on us.

It will not harm us to get rained on in summer unless we are going to be away from base for a long time. Clothes can be changed and, if the day is not too cold, they will dry on us as we walk. We can enjoy the feel of droplets landing on our skin, the rivulets of water running down our faces, the heaviness of clothes soaking up the rain. It will not harm us to feel the power of wind, buffeting us and blowing up clouds of sand or chaff or dead leaves around us. Walking under swaying trees and hearing the creaking branches as they rub on one another, we can feel energised by the brewing storm. It will not harm us to go out for a walk on a cold crisp morning, and feel the ice cold air reddening our faces, our breath frosting on our woollen scarves. It can be exhilarating to tramp on numbing feet through snow or to fish shards of ice out of a frozen pond in order to skim them across the surface. In all these we encounter the solid reality of the earth.

We get hot and perspire, we get cold and shiver. Our bodies change colour with temperature and abrasions. Insects bite and itch and form lumps on us. Brambles catch our ankles. Mostly, though, we keep a comfortable equilibrium. In short, we survive.

If we are frightened of the phenomena which make up the natural environment, we will not engage, but instead will keep ourselves within a protective bubble of modern life. Fear of reality lies at the root of many psychological problems. We live in ways which distance us from experiencing our vulnerability. We are afraid of our own mortality and the prospect of losing things which we love and which are important to us, so we create psychological layers of insulation against thinking about these possible losses. Even when we know that we cannot prevent the inevitable, we block it out of our minds.

Our attempts to stay comfortable in the outdoors may, at least in part, reflect anxieties of this kind, for in our contact with nature we are reminded of the basic fragility of life as well as of its beauty. We experience directly the frailties of our bodies as we test them in challenging circumstances. We see the enormity of forces which we are up against. At the same time, in experiencing the natural world, we also discover reassurance. Life regenerates and grows even in the shadow of death and decay. Once we let go and stop trying to avoid it, we discover that the process of life is trustworthy.

Refuge

The act of becoming Buddhist is called taking refuge. Taking refuge means connecting with a source of support, or, to understand the term more properly, allowing oneself to be held by that in which we take refuge. We can take refuge in ordinary things, like the bottle of wine or a relationship or ideas, and most people have such mundane sources of support on which they rely in times of stress, but this is not necessarily a healthy process. In

Buddhism, however, we take refuge in the spiritual dimension of our lives. We move out of the ordinary, small orbit of day to day concerns and deliberately found our lives on the universal truths which underpin them.

As a person makes the commitment of taking refuge, in Buddhism they traditionally commit to three things: Buddha, Dharma and Sangha. Other religious systems have similar acts of commitment and these often have similar elements.

Although they are Buddhist terms, the three refuges speak of fundamental truth which goes beyond particular religious systems. It is therefore useful to explore these ideas whether one is Buddhist or not. Exploring the meaning of the refuges is a lifelong project. It is often said that Buddhism starts and finishes with the refuges, for, although one starts by making the commitment with sincere intention, it is said that only when one reaches the highest levels of insight does one start to really understand them. So, here, I will attempt an interim discussion of their meaning. I think these concepts are useful to our exploration of working with the environment, as I will try to show.

When a person formally becomes Buddhist, the first refuge which they take is in Buddha. The Buddha was the historic founder of the religion, the teacher and the source. He was a great sage who lived 2500 years ago, a man who lived a homeless life, travelling the roads of Northern India, teaching in forests and parks and wild places. He lived and taught in harmony with his surroundings. So, at a simple level, in working with the environment, we can respect and take refuge in his example.

But also, a Buddha is the one who is capable of enlightening us. To become enlightened means giving up our self-centredness completely. It means seeing things as they are, not in a self-interested way. Working with the natural environment, we aim to engage with the world more fully, to encounter life in new ways and to challenge our habitual ways of seeing things. If we engage in an other-centred way, we stop seeing the world as functional to our personal needs, and appreciate it for what it is. When this happens, the natural world speaks to us and we start to listen. Thus, nature has the capacity to awaken us from our self-preoccupation. It becomes Buddha for us.

The second refuge is in Dharma. Dharma is the word that describes the Buddhist teachings, but it also means the foundational truth of all things. As we explore the environment and investigate many manifestations of life in its ever-changing intricacy, we discover its truth. Looking into nature, the natural world becomes a book which is constantly informative and educational. We see, we listen, we learn, in the immediate sense of the myriad beautiful insights and experiences which it gives us; but also, more profoundly, in the lessons it gives on the fundamental qualities of all things and of life. Dharma is also that which holds. When we take refuge in Dharma, we touch the earth and feel its solidity. We experience it as a manifestation of the unconditioned truth upon which life rests, which is so big that we only glimpse it, yet which we know experientially is there if we can let go and trust enough.

The third refuge is in sangha, the Buddhist community, or the community of practitioners. It is the group of fellow travellers on the spiritual way, who share with us and support our spiritual needs. As we touch more deeply into the natural world, we ground our lives in a sense of connection to other beings, both human and animal. Buddhism makes far less distinction between humans and animals than other religions. We are all on the same spiritual journey, even if we travel in different ways and are at different stages. Buddhists commonly speak of saving all sentient beings. So as we connect to nature, the world becomes our sangha and the creatures who inhabit it become our brothers. They are our spiritual friends, our teachers and our companions. Embraced by their love, we in turn learn to love others.

When we take refuge we bow down and touch the earth. Our bodies bend to the ground and rest upon it. The experience of touching the earth is one of letting go. As the body relaxes onto the soil, it feels the ground's solidity. We come to know experientially that we are held, even when we try to cling to nothing. This is the true experience of refuge.

Lying upon the earth and letting go, whether in refuge or a relaxation exercise, or simply resting on the lawn on a summer afternoon, we find ourselves deeply at peace. It is a homecoming.

For many people, the natural world is a place of safety, inspiration and solace. Sahishnu, one of the Amida Order members, writes:

Nature was my refuge long before [I became Buddhist]. It was where I ran and hid as a frightened child. As I sat at the top of a tree my problems came into perspective. The tree was there before me and would be there after I was long gone. I was but a tiny crumb, insignificant in the scheme of things.

As a teenager, I fled back to the countryside on my scooter. At night I sat for hours on a bank overlooking our small market town. The stars wheeled above and window lights [shone] below, inhabitants behind closed curtains. I felt I had more in common with the stars than those behind the curtains. Later, when trapped behind windows, streets and cities, I would rarely escape to walk in a cathedral of trees.

Being born in the country, I do not romanticise it. What I love or loved was the impersonal nature of nature, the great democracy of nature. What is worrying is the human tendency to try to turn it into a human tyranny, as if we are different. We are lemming-like, rushing towards our end. Nature restores balance with inconvenient droughts, floods, earthquakes, volcanoes and tsunamis. Except for our spirituality we truly are insignificant beings.

Psychology and spirituality

How can we be psychologically healthy if we are not spiritually alive and thriving? How can we be spiritually growing if we are bogged down in mental conflicts and compulsions? To try to separate something which we call psychological from what we call spiritual is a false dichotomy, for our whole being is founded on our spiritual nature. What we believe, what we trust, what we take refuge in, whether we live ethically, are all conditions which create our mental states of joy or suffering.

Buddhism is often represented as a psychological religion. The Buddha understood how much of our suffering is produced through our mental struggles, a result of our attempts to avoid things which we imagine to be unpleasant and which we would rather not know. Such compulsive avoidance of the truth creates the dulled mental state referred to as *avidya*, often translated as delusion, but more accurately meaning 'not seeing'. All good religious and spiritual practice is concerned with aligning our lives with higher purposes and the ground of truth, and this purpose is overtly explained in Buddhism in its understanding of the way that our minds are conditioned and its hope that we can get beyond that conditioning.

Psychologies also try to understand the ground of our minds, and in doing so to create firm foundations for mental health. They try to help us to be more open to experience as it arrives, to be in the flow of life rather than hiding from it in neuroses. They try to help us to work through the veil of projections, the transferences and obsessive preoccupations which cloud our view of others.

Thus both spiritual traditions and psychological ones are, in their various ways, concerned with helping us to live more at peace with the foundational truths of our lives: our mortality, our vulnerability, our failures in love and courage and our fears. They are about helping us to trust the ground of our being which is the ground of all beings, the ground of life itself.

So, in writing this book about working in the natural environment, I find myself treading ground which belongs both to psychology and to the spiritual. The two are inseparable. Exploring nature we are brought directly into contact with the most fundamental aspects of life, the joy of growth and regeneration, the omnipresence of death and decay. We see our lives in the context of a web of processes of which we are a tiny, and often problematic, part. We feel the impact of these facts upon us and we are affected by them. We are changed.

Deep ecology and therapeutic process

Many therapies are human-centric, giving virtually no attention to the larger ecological picture, but once we start to look at nature and involve it in our therapeutic work, we cannot help but be affected and concerned by knowledge of the way human activity impacts upon our planet. We are implicated in the unfolding troubles of the environment and this must impact upon our mental states.

This book is not particularly focused on global ecological or environmental issues, at least in an overt way. Its focus is on our spiritual and psychological relationship with the natural world at a more day to day level and on ways of facilitating intimacy with our environment. But it is impossible to do this work without an awareness of the issues which face us at this point in time, or the voices of those within the deep ecology movement, and other spiritually based environmental groups, who connect the trauma of watching our planet's problems with their sense of the spiritual dimension, and who feel grief, compassion and contrition for the actions of the human race when faced with the prospect of environmental disaster.

As we connect with the natural world, we find ourselves increasing our sensitivity to these issues naturally, and wanting to tread more lightly on the planet. As we grow and let go of compulsiveness we have less desire to consume, and start to approach life more gently. We come to understand how greed and consumption are psychologically driven.

In coming to love our local environments, we begin to live in ways which support them rather than undermining them. Ultimately, this kind of work may be as effective in bringing about a planetary change of consciousness as more direct communication of political and social messages. A change of heart leads to a change in action.

Of course we need to discuss and debate the issues, but this dialogue often takes place among those already converted, working out the finer points in strategies. The sort of environmental encounter described in this book takes another route and reaches other groups of people.

So our work is grounded in a deep understanding of our position as part of the eco-system. We are not as special as we think. Or perhaps it would be more accurate to say that everything, including ourselves, is far more special than we ever imagine in our day to day lives. We are recipients of the great privilege of life, sharing this world with a truly amazing assemblage of beings. Once we understand this deeply, knowing it in our bodies and our perception, we discover that in fact we live in the arms of a wonderful process of nature, of life. We might call it love.

Chapter Two

Other-Centred Approach and Environmental Therapy

Other-Centred Approach is grounded in Buddhist psychology. Buddhism offers a system of theory and methodologies for understanding mental process. This system is subtle and complex, and it offers a practical interpretation of the way that we try to deal with the realities of the ordinary and extraordinary difficulties and dangers which life brings by trying to create an illusion of permanence and security for ourselves which does not actually exist. We create a feeling of being in control of our lives by psychologically and practically clinging on to things which support our view of the world. This gives the impression that things do not change, even when in fact they do, and means that we feel less vulnerable to losses and personal dangers than we are, but it also prevents us from being fully alive. We deaden our perceptions and limit our actions to habitual ways of thinking and behaving.

This understanding of human process offers a valuable model for doing environmental work. Whilst we may try to control our experience and filter the information which our senses convey, opening up to new experiences and allowing things to impact upon us expands our limitations and challenges our habit patterns, and in working with the environment this sort of challenge happens all the time. Other-centred approach offers a model which can provide an integrating methodology and theory base for environmental therapies. It provides a perspective which not only provides rationale for the types of work which many therapists are already doing, but also suggests how that work can be extended and enhanced. It is a fully integrated system, which stands on its own, useful whether or not the Buddhist roots are made explicit.

With this in mind, this chapter will set out some of the basic theory of other-centred approach and show how it can create a foundation for this way of working. As such, it is the most theoretical chapter in the book. It is offered early to provide a framework for understanding subsequent chapters, but as reader, if you are more practically orientated, as many in this field are, you may choose to skip over this chapter for the present, referring back to it at a later stage or when a point needs clarifying. On the other hand, this chapter also offers a theoretical overview, and, in this way, provides a model which integrates and locates the material found in subsequent chapters.

Other-centred therapy

When we connect with others we change. Our way of thinking and being is subtly challenged and our world view is brought into question because we come to understand that their way of being and thinking is different from ours and they see the world through different eyes.

Buddhism understands the basic human problem to be rooted in our rigidities of thought, and of the way we perceive the world and relate to it. We do not just inhabit the world or relate to others, but rather, we psychologically appropriate what we see for our personal project. We identify with things or reject them, view them in particular ways or overlook them in order to confirm our personal view of the world.

We are afraid of those things in life which we cannot control and so we try to gain a sense of control by recreating the world around us in the image of worlds we have known before. We bring our assumptions and prejudices into our day to day inter-actions and, without even knowing it, we seek out the familiar and the confirmatory even in new surroundings.

We fear impermanence and loss, particularly because we fear sickness, our own deaths and the deaths of those we love, and we therefore try to create an illusion of permanence by automatically adjusting our experience to fit our pre-existing blueprint.

The core Buddhist teachings describe a psychology in which the mind is conditioned. A sense of self is created and maintained through cyclical processes of perception. These rely upon our capacity to seek out and adjust experience that is self-confirmatory.

Other-centred therapy is grounded in this Buddhist understanding. Like any serious therapy, it offers complexity in its approach. Other-centred therapy, however, differs from many other therapies in as much as its bias is towards relatedness and engagement rather than introspection. It primarily concerns itself with the person's perception of and relationship to others. In this therapy, the client is encouraged to enquire into his or her relatedness. This enquiry can take many forms, but broadly falls into two modalities: the first focusing on conditioned view (*rupa*) and the second on reaching beyond the conditioning, or, more properly stated, allowing the unconditioned to reach us. We will explore these two modalities later in this chapter.

There are real others. People and things, are not a part of us. Technically, we say that the world is made up of non-self elements. It is not just part of our mental structuring, functioning in order to support our sense of personal solidity, but, although this is obvious, we treat it as if it were. Even we are non-self if you want to get pedantic, but we are very much attached to the idea that we *are* self, and as such to seeing ourselves as a special case.

Because the identity is both the defence, and the source of our limitations, changing our attachment to being a special case provides the route to better psychological health. We will not eliminate the sense of self, and nor would this be desirable for people in the ordinary way of things, but rather we try to shift the focus of the client's attention onto engagement with others so that the identity naturally becomes less rigid and more open to changing with new experiences.

In developing the methodology associated with other-centred approach we[1] have found that, because of the strong attachment to identity, there is less mileage in pursuing the direction of challenging a person's sense of self and feelings of personal entitlement directly, even when these are problematic. Accepting that others have real feelings and thoughts which do not necessarily correspond to one's own, and looking for evidence of inconsistencies and assumptions in the world view, however, do provide ways to challenge self-preoccupation. This makes for a more effective therapeutic or spiritual strategy.

Other-centred approach focuses on the world view, not the self-view, aiming to facilitate a more realistic relationship with the world, which will in turn create better mental health. Some Western therapies are moving in similar directions based on evidence from studies of mental health, but other-centred approach offers a rationale for this direction based on a psychological model of mental construction.

So, other-centred work focuses on exploring perception. On the one hand it helps the person to see that their view of others, specific others that is, is distorted by many factors including history and context. On the other hand it sets up a line of enquiry in which the client is encouraged to question their assumptions and stories about the world and about those others who are important in their life. In so doing, the client gains empathy for those others. He or she learns to listen more deeply and to be open to new perspectives and new voices.

This foundation is one I have explored in more detail elsewhere (particularly in my recent book *Other-Centred Therapy*)[2] and it can be applied in many ways. Specifically though, we can relate it to work with the environment.

Going forth into nature

When we go out into nature we are surrounded by a world which offers us many rich experiences. In considering an approach to this sort of work within a Buddhist framework, we cannot ignore the fact that the Buddha and his followers spent much time in natural surroundings. Natural things are central to some of the key stories about the Buddha's life. For example, the Buddha was born, enlightened, taught and died under trees. He was sheltered by a cobra[3] and encountered many creatures from insects to wild elephants in his meditations.[4] He taught in nature images. We can read of the simile of the snake,[5] the parable of the herbs,[6] and the dream of the anthill.[7] He taught care for living things, both plants and animals.[8] He spent much time in forest groves and preached in a deer park. The Buddha sat on the ground to meditate and touched the earth as witness to his enlightenment. His cushion was grass and he slept on hay.

Leaving the urban life of luxury, the Buddha encountered the realities of impermanence, symbolised in the images of the Four Sights: a sick person, an old person, a dead person and a holy man. He faced his fear of the forest, deliberately cultivating determination and persistence as he described in The Sutta on Fear and Dread.[9] So it was that he came to spiritual insight. It was through seeing the world beyond his palace that he awoke to the spiritual truth.

In some of the accounts given in the Buddhist texts, the nature images are central to the story, but in many they are not particularly emphasised. The natural world is, for the most part, the scenery of the stories in the sutras rather than their action focus. The forest dwelling experience was so intrinsic to the spiritual life of the time that the early followers of the Buddha lived that it is taken for granted in the texts, but it is there, a backdrop to the storyline. Natural imagery and forest places form the setting for events and the resources for the spiritual community.

Embodied experience and grounding

The creation of delusion and the building of a self-orientated world view is, in Buddhist theory, mediated by the senses. The senses connect us to the world. Observing the actions of the senses can be particularly important to other-centred work since they are the interface with others.

The senses are themselves conditioned. Each has its own tendencies to act in ways that support self-creation.

The senses are attracted to things, or, put technically, 'objects', that confirm or point to the self. Called *the uncontrollables*, the senses are caught by objects which fascinate and draw the attention because they support the habitual preoccupations of the self-story. Understanding how the different senses each play a role in the creation and maintenance of the self can offer insights in any therapeutic work, but working with this sense attachment process is particularly helpful for environmental work since exposure to the environment creates so many opportunities for observing the action of the senses.

As we saw in the previous chapter, in interacting with the natural world we begin with grounding exercises. These bring our attention to our senses in an immediate way. In particular, they invite us to give attention to the body sense, so often ignored by the intellect based mind. We interrupt the habitual bias towards sight and sound whilst sensing the earth, the air and our embodied nature through the sense of touch. Grounding brings a heightened awareness of all the senses since it creates a state of embodied attention, but it particularly develops the sense of touch. It takes us out of our normal patterns of thinking and counters any tendency to avoid those things which are most immediate to us. We can also bring the same detailed attention specifically to the other senses, using exercises which focus on sight or sound or smell. We can learn to look and listen afresh.

The emphasis on embodied experience is also important because the mediation of experience not only takes place through the senses, but also through our reaction to what we perceive. This reaction is embodied. In Buddhist psychology the creation of self is seen as taking place through a cycle of conditioned perception and response.

The cycle begins with perception. Our attention is caught by the power of certain objects. This power is basically a function of the object's ability to condition our sense of self, and it is called *rupa*. *Rupa* is not the object itself but our perception of the object and specifically the power that the object has to hold our attention. When we perceive the object which is *rupa* for us, we react to it.

When we react to an object, this reaction takes us to the next stage in the cycle. We see something and react to it because it has associations for us. By making these associations, we structure our mentality. The creation of habitual mental structures is called *samskara,* commonly referred to as mental formation. Mental formation conditions our intentionality, which in turn conditions the focus of our attention. It leads us to view the world in a conditioned way and to seek out objects and perceptions which confirm our sense of self.

These processes and the teachings which elaborate them are described in more detail in my earlier books.[10] It is probably not necessary to understand them in depth to appreciate the approaches in this book, unless you wish to deepen the theoretical basis of your work.

The cyclical process of self-creation is presented in several different Buddhist teachings, one of which is a teaching called the *skandhas*. This teaching describes the cycle of self-creation using a five stage model. In this teaching, the first step is *rupa* and the second step in the process, *vedanā*.

Vedanā is embodied reaction.[11] This embodied reaction is the step in the process whereby the self-based mentality grasps onto or rejects the experience of the senses and thus creates the distortions of experience which bring our experience of the world into line with the self-story. By grasping some experiences and rejecting other experiences, we filter our contact with the world, choosing to identify with those things which support our sense of identity and to reject those which do not. The reaction is immediate, pre-cognitive and visceral, like an amoeba grasping its food or pulling away from unpleasant objects.

Being more aware of the body sense, therefore, we are more likely to catch and observe these processes as they happen. Slowing down the body, we interrupt the habitual processes as they happen. This is helpful because the next stage in the *skandha* process involves getting hooked into habitual scripts. Once we have got caught up in an old script it is much harder to see how we are limiting our response to the world. Once we are caught in an old script, we become entranced by it, losing objectivity and awareness that we are acting in programmed ways.

Listening to the body sense, we can become more aware of our patterns of selective perception and reaction. It also slows us down and creates mental space for this sort of awareness. The mind tends to chatter on, preventing us from giving attention to our immediate experience.

The body has always been the focus for developing meditative awareness. Stilling the body, the practitioner stills the mind. So too in stopping the rush of mental activity by giving attention to the body sense, the therapy client quietens those voices which persist in repeating old scripts, and listens to what arises spontaneously.

For all these reasons giving attention to the body is a valuable preliminary to environmental work. In addition to developing awareness of the body, though, a fundamental Buddhist practice is to give awareness to the ground itself, and this importance translates to other-centred work. Touching the earth, we connect with the planet, and in bringing awareness to this connection we appreciate our dependence on her providence.

Touching the earth is formalised in many spiritual practices.

We sit in meditation on the floor. We do walking meditation, slowly, planting our feet with awareness. We prostrate ourselves on the ground, bowing and stretching ourselves out and giving ourselves to the earth. We take refuge by placing ourselves in the arms of the Buddha and in the belly of the earth.

So, in grounding exercises, we bring our awareness to this earth connection. We slow down and centre ourselves, and we touch the great expanse of the planet on which we walk and can rely. We feel in our bodies the daily faith of walking step by step.

Two directions

Other-Centred Therapy[12] works with our relatedness to others. Its methodology is based on a principle that we can work with two aspects of this experience.

Firstly, our view of others and the ways in which we relate to them is conditioned. Others are *rupa* for us. That is, we perceive them in ways that are driven by the power that they have to support our sense of self. The *rupa* aspect of experience can be explored in terms of different factors of conditioning: our histories, our interests, our sense of who we are and what groups we associate with, our culture and its mythologies as well as the immediate precursors to the situation.[13] In our exploration of the client's world view we can unpick the origins of the *rupa* quality, seeing how we came to view things in a particular way as a result of past experience, and we can look at how the rupa process is maintained and continues to support particular ways of seeing things.

The other direction of therapeutic exploration is to bring into question the *rupa* aspect of perception and to explore the reality of the objects and people we encounter. This involves allowing others to speak to us in various ways, as much as it involves trying to understand them. When we get our selves out of the way, we listen better and see better. We can help this process in two ways: by directly questioning the truth of our perceptions, or by investigating the world with greater attention. Instead of just enquiring into our own process, we can develop empathy for others. In broad, all Buddhist therapies aim to reduce the hold of self-structures and create a more fluid, open relationship with the world. Other-centred approach does this by focusing on other people, things and places and our relatedness to them.

Environmental therapy can reflect both aspects of other-centred work. Other-centred environmental work may explore and work with the conditioned way that we experience wild things and it can also work with exploring the reality which is masked by this conditioned view. Often both aspects of the work unfold alongside one another, for, in meeting the natural world, we may become more aware both of our interpretations and also of how these are disrupted by the reality of what we are experiencing. Most importantly, we allow the environment to speak to us.

Conditioned view

People often have preconceptions about the natural world. They may have fears and resistances to wild spaces or romantic notions about living in harmony with nature, and these may become apparent before a group has even started work. If the therapy group meets for a preliminary session indoors before going out into nature, talking about expectations will not only help to prepare group members for the experience, but also to reveal some of the mental processes which are colouring their view.

Unrealistic expectations may manifest in things like unrealistic choices of clothes and equipment, questions about what risks the group will be facing, specific worries, or stories about dramatic past experiences. At this stage simply hearing and reflecting these concerns is usually enough. It is good to give opportunities for such anxieties to be voiced, but it is also wise to limit the process, as too much discussion tends to build unrealistic fantasies and fuel anxieties unnecessarily. Nature herself will be the real teacher.

In some cases, group members will be interviewed by facilitators in advance. This is appropriate in settings where participants are from an unknown setting or have specific needs or difficulties. Their fears or expectations may be voiced in this process. As group facilitator you may choose to respond to concerns directly at this point, or may prefer to say nothing. Unless the person is dangerously unequipped or likely to find solitary aspects of the work too unsettling, it may be best to rely on learning naturally emerging.

In the field, conditioned view becomes apparent in choices which are made. A person may choose particular types of working space repeatedly or be preoccupied with certain aspects of the work. It will also manifest in the stories and associations which are emerge from the process. Some of these stories may be historic and relate to life experiences in childhood and more recent times. Other associations may be more symbolic or may represent things which are significant in the person's current life.

The same place will feel different for different members of the group depending on these factors. For example, dark places might feel spooky and evoke feelings of fear and apprehension for some people, whilst feeling comfortable and private for others. In the extreme, going into dark woods might have particular associations with bad memories of childhood abuse or wartime incidents for some. Such an association could lead to strong reactions and even flash-backs, so facilitators need to be a little wary and take a group into situations step by step until they know their group members well enough to have a sense of what might be unleashed. Nevertheless, in such circumstances, encountering the real wood in the present setting may be a potent source of healing if handled with sensitivity. Mostly, though, associations are more subtle and amenable to exploration.

Different reactions will be influenced by people's individual histories and psychological make-up but they will also be influenced by the stage a group is at in its process.[14] Giving space to express and explore these associations can be valuable. The group may want to share personal material of this kind in gatherings or other group formats, though, as we will see, talking is not always necessary or therapeutic.

Metaphoric work is common in therapy. Natural places lend themselves to exploring metaphor. Metaphoric work is an extension of *rupa* enquiry. Environmental work can be imaginative and creative in many different ways. One might, for example, imagine a stone heap as a futuristic city and develop stories about the lives of its inhabitants. One might even create drama playing out such tales, set in a natural location. Such exercises are fun and creative, but they also challenge and disrupt rigid patterns of thinking. The group sees beyond the 'piles of old stones' and discovers new possibilities in it.

This sort of work can use a wide variety of styles and media: writing or music making, building large scale earth sculptures or other visual arts. The materials themselves can come from nature, giving a rich experience of interaction with its physicality. 'Found' objects increase our sensitivity to texture and shape. Other-centred methods encourage the development of empathy for materials. This can be done by introducing awareness exercises before starting work. Practical interaction with the environment can help to release people from inhibitions around creativity in ways which creative work using commercial art materials might not.

Shamanic work takes imaginative work a stage further, involving the use of altered states, mental journeying and ritual. The practice of undertaking a vision quest inspires some more intensive types of outdoor experience. There are precedents for this sort of work in a number of Buddhist schools and practices as well as in Native American and other cultures. Intensive practice, whether undertaken in a remote hermitage, cave or temple, or whilst walking from place to place, is often done with a hope of achieving visionary experiences.

All these methods can be integrated into an other-centred framework. They help the participant explore and enrich their personal world of association and imagery and discover shared metaphor and myth, common to their own and other cultures. In some cases the work can be inspirational, touching both spiritual and psychological aspects of life, involving transpersonal as well as personal material.[15] At its most powerful, working with the environment involves direct spiritual or religious encounter, facilitated by the natural awe which life inspires.

Encounter with nature

In environmental work, I personally prefer to work in ways which involve an immersion in nature over a period of several days rather than working with a series of short sessions, but both formats are possible. The choice of formats usually depends on the constraints of the situation in which a group is set up.

With a longer encounter, change emerges naturally. Participants discover new ways of relating to the environment as the world speaks directly to them, mediated by a series of different exercises which build into a natural sequence. If the process can unfold uninterrupted, there is little need for verbal processing because each experience leads on from the last. In shorter sessions, however, each session will need to be given closure and there will be more of a tendency toward discussing experiences at the end of each occasion. This probably means that in a particular session only one or two activities can take place before a verbal discussion is needed.

Other-centred work can take the form of detailed enquiry. During the eco-therapy week, for example, we used an exercise to investigate the lives of ants living in the field where we were working. We watched the ants on several occasions, observing them scuttling through the leaf mould under the oak trees, carrying various objects along their established routes. The observations raised many questions about the lives of ants. They also led group members to make comparisons with human society. Participants were amazed, for example, by the size of some of the bigger anthills in the field, which towered a foot or two above the grass. Relative to the size of the ants, these were equivalent to the size of a mountain on a human scale.

Letting go of the human perspective a little, it becomes possible to see the world from the position of a creature of very different size and needs, but also we realise how much we can never know about the ant's perspective. It is a sobering reminder of our species-based preoccupations and human-centric approach to the planet.

Other-centred work can involve developing the use of different senses. Switching from the habitual sense modality can lead to intensified experience as the new sense is less heavily conditioned. For example, listening to birdsong in the early morning whilst meditating out of doors, we hear more sharply and appreciate the purity of the notes in the clear air. Walking blindfolded, guided by a partner increases a person's awareness of the contours of the ground. Small irregularities in the surface, such as clumps of grass or cut stumps of cleared undergrowth, which would normally be barely felt, become potential obstacles.

In one exercise, participants chose a stone and investigated it with their hands with their eyes closed, then added it to a pile in the centre of the group. They then tried to find the same stone by touch. This exercise involves using the hands to observe small differences of shape and texture. It frequently evokes strong feelings of identification and possessiveness, which we can look at in a light-hearted way.

Such activities intensify awareness and improve our skill in giving attention, rather like playing scales in music. They hone the capacity to observe in new ways. But more importantly, exposure to nature brings many encounters which cannot be engineered or planned. A morning alone in the wood brings many meetings with wildlife large and small. A night lying in the field beneath the stars evokes wonderment, which is intensified by the stream of a meteor crossing the sky. Encountering the extraordinary, as well as finding the ordinary beauty of the countryside, changes people. The freshness of growing things, the scent of decay in a wood, the solidity of rocks and the different qualities of light as hours pass and weather changes touch us. Encountering life and death, growth and change, we experience things which are sometimes disturbing and other times uplifting, but always grounding. It is hard to remain withdrawn from life for long whilst meeting with nature and the impact of such experiences is developed by the reflective context of a group.

Ancestry

Encountering nature embeds us in the present. We are fully alive in each moment of experience. It also has the potential to connect us with the past. When we face the natural world, we are not so caught in the humdrum personal stories of our small lives, but, rather, we begin to appreciate the shared ground of our ancestors who, generation by generation, walked the same tracks and watched the same sky. Adopting simpler ways, living in wild places, we begin to understand the basic human relationship with the earth. We appreciate growing food and building with local stone and timber, gathering wood and making fires. Living outside we look beyond our modern appliances and comfortable houses and see the basic work and tools on which human survival depends. We maybe also come to appreciate a little the way that many in the world still live, cooking on wood fires out of doors with a minimum of pots and pans and scavenged wood, and living in tents or huts or in the open, though for us it is play rather than necessity to live this way.

At a deeper level we come to appreciate our part in the life of the planet itself. We recognise our commonality with animals, as well as our differences, our genetic and cultural inheritances. With this recognition we start to become less attached to a human-centred viewpoint. Just as individually we tend to base our world view on personal identity and the self-world, so too, at a collective level, we view the universe from a human perspective. We see everything in terms of our collective human needs and definitions. We divide the world into countries, but these are meaningless to birds or animals which cross their borders. We buy and sell land, but never ask the consent of the other creatures that live upon it. As humans we are strongly territorial, just as robins or chimpanzees or cats, but through working with the natural environment, we start to hold our maps more provisionally and respect their limitations.

Working with and without words
The environment is a rich resource for sanity and health. Deeply therapeutic, the work transcends what is ordinarily thought of as therapy. Much is done without interpretation. Insight is often regarded as important in therapeutic process, and putting such insight into words is often seen as valuable, but in environmental work it can be more important not to get caught up in words. Part of the reason for this is that words tend to concretise experience. They also create distance. By naming and describing things, we start to put our stamp on to them and perceive them through our habitual viewpoints, thus cutting ourselves off by closing our minds in various ways. We also fix them and create rigidity in our thinking and perception

Sometimes words are helpful to the process of engaging. Finding words to talk about the ants or the stars or the cooking can make us look more carefully at things which we have maybe overlooked before. The words can sharpen observation. Talking in generalities or about our self experience, on the other hand, may be less helpful as it draws us back into self-interest and abstraction.

The distinction between the helpful and unhelpful use of words is primarily based on whether the words are self-focused or other-focused. Creativity with words can be immensely enriching, for example in poetry or descriptive writing. Struggling to find words for the exact colour and shape of a leaf or the angle of bend of the tree branch or trying to convey what it is like to watch the sun set, or hear the sound of a deer bellowing in the night forces us to return to the experience which we are describing and look more closely, more attentively.

Writing things down may also reveal the shortcomings of observation and memory. Try writing about a place which you know, describing it in as much detail as you can muster from memory, then return to the place and see just how many things you have omitted. Probably many of these omissions were not only missing from the written account, but also not even remembered. Many times in writing this book I have been struck by how, even when I thought I was describing a scene accurately, I actually missed out significant details. On returning to the place where the event which I was describing occurred, I would find that some feature of it was completely missing from my account.

In much therapeutic work of this kind, however, verbal interpretation of the experience is better avoided. Such reflection can reduce processes which are fluid to static concepts, concretising interpretations and losing layers of experience which are tentative and subtle. Whilst there is a place for analysis and understanding, these reflections are better kept until later in the overall process. If they occur too early, they may pre-empt experience, establishing explanations and stories before they unfold naturally.

The self-story is very pervasive and all too easily we fall into telling and retelling the out-of-date versions of our lives, clothing them in new forms but preserving our habitual patterns of thinking and interpretation. As new situations arise, our descriptions of them to ourselves and to others adjust the experiences and fit them into old categories. This is why we enjoy recounting our adventures over and over.

So telling the story of the group may be better left until a late stage. This gives time for different versions of the experience to emerge and fall away and the natural world to reiterate its messages without them being continually attached to the self-story.

Sacred Space

Other-centred work rests upon an appreciation that encounter with what is really other is the ground of spiritual truth. In Buddhist terminology it is Dharmic. The real other is the unconditioned. It is beyond self, so has the nature of Buddha, the capacity to awaken us. Whether we approach this work from a Buddhist perspective or some other foundation, this spiritual truth remains. Encountering nature, we come face to face with the deep truth of existence, its perpetual recreation and its spiritual quality. We are in relation to that unconditioned other, and although our perception of it is conditioned and limited, we still experience its reality to some degree beyond that conditioning.

On this basis, the environment offers a place of refuge and of spiritual discovery. As we meet the complexity and mystery of nature and of all the unfolding processes of birth and death which she embraces, we are brought into direct contact with the sacred. We touch the measureless and the universal.

Thus, in working with nature, we work with sacred space. We enter into and celebrate the wonder of life in all its forms and the dependent and interdependent nature of its being. We come to appreciate deeply our own vulnerability and dependence upon the earth and all the conditions which it provides. We stand in awe of the universe in its immensity. We face the questions that humankind has faced for millennia.

Ways forward

The other-centred approach offers environmental therapies a theoretical model founded on an appreciation of reality. It asserts the respect-worthiness of life in its various forms.

Within this model a wide range of techniques can be integrated. The model recognises that we have conditioned perception, but also takes into account the foundational otherness of reality. It integrates both projective and exploratory work, allowing them to sit side by side. The inevitably surprising quality of experience in environmental work unsettles our habitual ways of interacting with life and challenges our outdated ways of seeing things. It gives birth to our creative spirit and demonstrates our habituation.

More though, environmental work creates space in which the natural world can speak to us. Sitting in a wood or uncut meadow, by a river or the sea, experiences arise which are not engineered, but arrive unbidden, gifts from the universe. The sight of a heron swooping low against a slate blue sky or tiny fishes leaping, like silver darts, above a mirror smooth lake surface at sunset, or a field mouse, caught in indecision as the brush cutter approaches, change us in increments which cannot be measured or accounted. This is therapy at its best.

This chapter has outlined some of the key characteristics of other-centred approach and some of the ways in which it can be applied to environmental work. In the following chapters we will revisit some of these themes and look in more detail at specific areas of working.

Chapter Three

Sacred Space

In the mornings we sit in the bamboo grove. The bamboo was planted the first year that we came to the centre in France. We bought it from the nursery on the road to Charenton. The man who sold it had forgotten that he had it, but there it was, tucked in among some other plants beside the car park.

It came in a pot, simply a few canes, standing shoulder height against me. We wondered how it would survive as we set it down at the end of the field, below the garden and some distance from the house. Lots of plants do not survive the winters here in France, for frosts can be severe and the house is often unoccupied for months at a time. The bamboo seemed so lost among the field grasses and blackthorn, a tiny oriental invasion in a European profusion of wildness. We watered it carefully all summer and left it in the autumn with some anxiety. We were delighted to return in the spring and find it still flourishing.

Bamboo grows underground, and, like mushrooms, throws up its stems into the air rather as an afterthought. Already formed, they extend with amazing rapidity, growing to full height in days. As such, it is a good metaphor for some types of spiritual life: subterranean growth, persistence, emerging into the world only after a long period of preparation as a flowering of shoots which are grounded in a well extended root system.

During the early years, growth was slow as the plant established itself, producing only a few new canes each year. We would water it carefully in dry weather and count how many stalks had been produced each season. Then suddenly, after about a decade, things changed. The whole clump seemed to suddenly take off into new growth. Shoots sprang through the bramble and thicket and ran in rambling lines across the field, too many to count. Big elongated cones, the growing tips of the new canes, emerged from the ground, poking up through the grass in unexpected places. The newest shoots grew bigger than before. Now the canes soared treelike above our heads, forming a canopy of fluttering leaves. The bamboo patch ceased to be a plant and became a space.

It is now seventeen years since we planted the bamboo. It continues to grow. We have cut a path that winds through the stems and forms part of our meditation walk in the mornings. There is even a shrine among the stalks to Quan Shi Yin, the female figure who represents compassion, with a small ring of stones circling a central larger slab and a tiny red resin figurine of the bodhisattva. It seems fitting to bring her female energy here amid the greenery. Bamboo exudes femininity, with its slender elegance and delicate foliage which belie its iron-strong stems and solid rootedness. Try to cut a bamboo cane and you soon discover it will not yield to anything but the sharpest saw. Try to uproot it, and you find it holds into the ground and onto its neighbours with the ferocity of a lioness guarding her brood.

Today we have come for morning meditation. All is silent. I am one of the first to arrive. Simon sits silently further into the clump, but he rises on seeing me, bringing me the small bell with which to mark the start and end of the formal session. We bow but do not speak. There is no need for words for each of us knows what is needed.

Gradually the other group members arrive. One by one, stepping carefully upon the earth as they walk, they pass me, entering the grove. I have chosen a spot near to the entrance, a space between the stems which is perfectly circular and just big enough for me to sit cross-legged upon the ground. There is no need for a cushion. The floor is warmly carpeted with fallen leaves, bleached to light beige: soft, smooth, elongated ellipses.

There are many such gaps among the canes now, for the plant creates a natural honeycomb of cells as its lead roots extend to colonise the space. There are enough for a dozen of us to each find a spot. We are separated by the stems, but yet connected, glimpsed sideways between the canes.

As people find their places, gradually the bamboo clump becomes alive with coloured forms. Bright fleeces, coloured hats, striped blankets interrupt the natural greens and browns of the plants, but the colours are softened and broken by the vertical lines of the canes.

Early sun, rising above the far hedgerow, sends shafts of light through the spaces, throwing the canes into an abstract collage of light and dark. Some stems are green, others, the older ones, have died, but still stand amongst the rest, golden brown or bleached light with time. Their surfaces are chiselled, striated with the lines of sinuous fibre, which broaden at the nodes where small side shoots emerge, forming dainty branches with thin fingers stretched outwards and fluttering leaves. Looking ahead, the eye is caught alternately by the beauty of these stem forms and the receding spaces between them: form and space, creating one another in infinitely varying fascination.

The group assembles. Slowing down, people reconnect with the place, and, in doing so, with one another. All is silent, but for the gently rustling as people settle themselves, oust awkward twigs that have fallen overnight and press into the sitting flesh, and wrap their blankets closer against the early chill. A single bell marks the start. All becomes quiet and still.

But stillness is not a natural quality of bamboo. As minds and bodies settle, the stems and leaves above our heads catch the slightest passing breath of wind, and flutter whisperings down to us as we sit at their feet. Nature has not heard of stillness and its meditation is the flow of life which constantly moves and changes. As we become quiet, the space is given to others. Small birds join us, their melodious, falling chant caressing our hearing senses. Insects hum and buzz around us, mostly harmlessly, but sometimes biting. The more stalwart among us sit on, the rest mindfully, or not so mindfully, brush them off. Far off the braying of a donkey and sounds of farm machines connect us to the world, too busy to waste time in quietude.

Then from the stillness, on a second bell we start our chant. We have become accustomed to using part of our time here for a practice of a thousand nembutsu. This chant seems particularly fitted to the bamboo. It is simple and repetitious, each person quietly but audibly repeating the call of longing, of gratitude, to the immeasurable Buddha, to the universal possibility of connection and love that we call Amida.

Namo Amida Bu, we chant, but it could be any chant which expresses our human embeddedness in the sacred, in the natural world, and in life. The sound rises like a murmur, like bees in a summer flowerbed, between the bamboo stems. We breathe nembutsus into the space and the space breathes them back to us in its own tongues. And in sharing this place we understand one another.

And gradually, softly as it began, the chant subsides. We fade back into the silence, and, as we cease our voices, we simply listen. The air is clear. Each sound glistens like a crystal in precise location. We feel each noise, hearing with skin as well as ears, goose-bumps of crackling leaves and caresses of birdsong. So we sit and breathe with the breath of the bamboo. Straight but yet fluid, still but yet dancing, we become what we already are, bathed in its exuberance.

Eventually we finish. A bell announces the end of the practice period. In silence we stand, collect our belongings, and then step out of our cells onto the path. Slowly, carefully, we walk. One foot follows the other, touching the earth with reverence at each step. Step following step, following step. Up through the field we walk, by the path that winds its way back towards the house. Past the row of runner beans at the end of the garden, past the row of potatoes, and through the gap in the dry-stone wall we go. Up into the yard between house and meditation hall we come, a line of practitioners, refreshed and enriched by an hour of sitting. The bamboo grove is empty of humans now. The sacred space remains, held by the plants.

Creating shrines

At the beginning of our week working with nature, Sundari and I discuss the possibility of creating some sort of shrine for the group. We have done this on other occasions when we have run eco-therapy groups. It has been a particularly lovely way to bring the group energy together and to dedicate it to spiritual ends. Creating a shrine does not necessarily mean making something religious. It does not have to be Buddhist or Christian or aligned with any particular tradition. It is simply a focus for the group's spiritual attention, a place where we bring together objects which represent the spiritual process for us individually or collectively.

Shrines have become popular again in our modern world. Whilst organised religion is, in many places, losing followers, some forms of spiritual activity are still very much alive. People are turning to other places for spiritual support. Old traditions seem to be resurfacing in new guises.

One familiar phenomenon is the roadside shrine. In France, as we drive, we pass many roadside crucifixes. Iron crosses supporting the dying figure of Christ lean out of small stone shelters, or stand, exposed to the elements, at crossroads. Sometimes there are flowers; simple bunches of garden blooms in jam jars, placed at His feet by pious locals. In other parts of France, more ancient Celtic stones, beaten by weather and time, still greet the wayfarer. For a long time people seemed to have forgotten how to create roadside shrines, but now modern shrines are beginning to appear once more. After an accident, it is now commonplace for people to lay flowers or leave messages at the place where the event occurred. Driving along country roads one passes many such impromptu displays of mourning.

Tragedies which are in the public eye bring larger displays. Many will remember the sea of flowers laid outside Kensington Palace when Princess Diana died, or the walls of messages created in New York and elsewhere after 9/11. Hospices and hospitals sometimes have unaligned shrines in their entrance halls or corridors, where relatives can place tributes to loved ones. They are places for memorials and prayers of hope. When I was in Hawaii a year or two ago, I saw a shop window in Hilo which had been given over as a community shrine. It was filled with all sorts of offerings and notes, remembrances and expressions of gratitude. Some were very touching. There were children's shoes and toys, and personal photographs of loved ones, presumably lost. All must have had meaning to the person or people who placed them there, and maybe to the community as a whole.

A shrine is a place that symbolises and represents a spiritual truth. It gives focus and energy to feelings which otherwise hover unexpressed, allowing people a point to which they can relate their spiritual impulses. It is a place of power. We use the word *rupa* to describe the figure on a Buddhist shrine. It is the same word as is used to describe the power which objects have to captivate the mind and distort our perception. This is because the shrine has the power to represent the spiritual realm to us, and thus hold spiritual energy for us. They can captivate our minds too.

The shrine is a representation of the holy, the focus for practice and devotion. It may be associated with a particular Buddha or deity, but it need not be limited in this way. Shrines can be primarily focused on the figure to which they are dedicated, but they can also be about an expression of a collective outpouring of spiritual sentiment. They can be about the object of worship to which they are dedicated or about the process of worshipping. In the latter form, they can embrace the experiences and needs of different people who have different beliefs and faith backgrounds but a common spiritual need. The latter sort of shrine expresses shared human experiences such as gratitude, longing or grief. They may be more or less secular and have more or less formality, depending on the needs of those who use them.

For a group which is not religiously aligned, the shrine which is expressive of spiritual need is more appropriate. In therapeutic work, group shrines are generally of this kind. The shrine can provide a location for personal work and meet participants' spiritual and psychological needs for sacred presence. It focuses the group's spiritual energies without needing to be affiliated in any way. A place of reverence, it can be somewhere to offer expressions of thankfulness or sorrow or a place to ask for support. It can meet broad spiritual needs as well as specific ones.

In the past, when we created shrines in therapeutic groups, Sundari and I invited people to go out into the natural environment and find objects which seemed meaningful to them, and then to bring them back to the group space. There we built our shrine, making it the focal point to the group. We added traditional items such as candles and flowers and used chants from different traditions as dedication. Creating a shrine at the end of the group brought closure and allowed us to honour the work we had done together.

Sacred space
In fact, this summer, as we start to discuss the possibility, Sundari and I decide not to create a shine. To make a shrine on this occasion would mean making one part of the site into the spiritual focus for the group. Since it is our intention to work in different locations all over the land, and to move from place to place, we want to develop the sense that each place has its own

spiritual energy. We want to honour the sacred which is to be found in the natural world all around us, so we want to develop the sense that the whole site is a sacred space within which we are living and working. Our whole week's activities will be enveloped and enclosed in the sacred, in the natural world, and in the presence of life and growth and love. So, on this occasion, we do not create a specific shrine. The whole site becomes our sacred space.

Whilst shrines create a focus towards which the ritual of spiritual practice is addressed, a sacred space is an area, boundaried and sanctified through ceremonial or ritual, within which spiritual activity takes place. A shrine is a place that we relate to, but a sacred space is entered and inhabited. The idea of sacred space is common to many religions and spiritual traditions. It is a space which is created in order to make things possible which are not possible in ordinary life. A liminal place, the sacred space sits between the ordinary and the mystery of the immeasurable.

In sacred spaces different rules operate. Whether through dictate or spontaneous recognition of the holy, when we enter into a sacred space we feel that we have crossed a boundary. Things are different.

Sometimes there is a clear line, a doorway or entrance which needs to be crossed. This may even involve some kind of gatekeeper, rites, or initiation. Other times we discover that we have stumbled into the presence of the divine almost by chance. We sense the special atmosphere. We pause, caught by the unexpected.

Whilst some sacred spaces are centred on shrines, a focus of this kind is not necessary, for the whole circle may be electrified with spiritual energy. In sacred spaces experience is magnified.

The therapeutic space can itself be viewed as a sacred space, bounded by the parameters of time and space within which the session takes place. Sundari and I reflect upon this. This week the boundaries of the group will create the threshold and the physical limits of the site will set its perimeter. Within this space the potency of work will be magnified by the level of attention and concentration in the group. Our plan is for an immersion experience so that the whole week is embraced by these parameters. Collectively, we are setting ourselves apart from the world and celebrating our relationship with the environment in which we are working. There will be 'down time', time for light conversation and fun, but all will happen within the context of the sacred circle.

Discovering sacred spaces

Although we can intentionally create sacred spaces, some places seem to naturally inspire us to thoughts of the spiritual. Waterfalls and mountains, sunsets and seascapes are commonly seen as spiritually inspiring. Some places of this kind become permanent sites of pilgrimage and religious association.

Sometimes too, a history of devotional practice contributes to the sense of the sacred. Near our centre in France there are many Romanesque churches dating back to the eleventh and twelfth centuries. They are ancient buildings, solid but simple in their architecture, places which are full of history, quietly confident about their secret pasts.

Often these old churches are themselves placed in locations which have great natural beauty. They sit on rocks perched above gorges, in deeply wooded valleys, or on rolling hills, visible from the surrounding countryside. Le Puy en Velay is in the south-east of the central Massif. The old town is dominated by three volcanic plugs; towers of rock that were once the lava cores of long extinct volcanoes. These dramatic features have clearly fascinated people for centuries and have inspired them spiritually. One of the rocks supports a fine, old church, another, a statue of the Virgin and the third a chapel.

The combination of human and natural environments at such

places seems to breathe spiritual meaning into the midst of ordinary life. One imagines that the creators of such buildings were themselves closely in touch with their environment and its spiritual qualities. The harmony between the old stone buildings and the rocks on which they stand suggests an appreciation of the relationship between humans and the natural world.

In the past people lived and died in close relationship with nature. Not in a romantic, distanced way, but integrating their lives with the seasons and with the earth. They lived close to the soil, growing or catching their own food and cutting wood from the forests. This experience of nature was so much a part of their world that it creeps into the architecture of medieval Europe in all sorts of ways. Carved bosses and the capitals of pillars in old churches are frequently embellished with plants and fruits, with creatures real and imagined, or with scenes of country life; planting and harvest, wood collecting and hunting. Pagan, pre-Christian symbols crop up too, hidden among the rafters or carved into the doorways or ornamentation of churches. The earlier worship based on this nature-focused world persisted and was incorporated into the new religion.

In our modern world, architects seem to know more of the urban environment than of the countryside, and buildings reflect modern preoccupations of speed and efficiency, style and convenience. There are exceptions though, and a growing generation of green builders is emerging, whose structures blend more sympathetically into the environment with exciting results. But these are unusual, creative ideas looking towards a future which is more in harmony with organic processes. For the moment they are out of the mainstream of city based life.

As modern people, we can still find inspiration in natural places. Last year I visited my friends Adrienne and Koyo Kubose in their house near the mountains of North California. After I had settled in, Koyo Sensei, a Pureland Buddhist minister, took me to look at the area around the house. We walked together around the land behind the bungalow, which is strewn with huge granite boulders and criss-crossed by small streams. Pine trees have grown up in the crevices between the rocks, creating tableaux which might come from Taoist paintings, and there is a constant sound of trickling water as rivulets find their way out of the sparse peaty soil, running between the mounds of stone, and creating a constant musical accompaniment.

The boulders are impressive. One in particular, which stands behind the house, is so big that it towers over the one-story building. When you climb to the top of it, which you can do by approaching it from behind, you can look down onto the house roof.

This rock has a particularly powerful quality to it, not least through its sheer size. Rev Kubose uses it as a backdrop for ordination ceremonies for his lay priests. It is a natural holy place, a shrine hewn by time and geological forces. He tells me that they bought the house for that rock. It is a magical place and it seems fitting for it to have become a religious centre.

Whilst some places have probably remained unchanged for centuries, their sacred energy seeming to come from the enduring quality of rock and earth, forged by the power of water, wind and fire, other places offer experiences which are transient, made up of light and air. One place of transience occurs at the end of each day. With the turning of the earth, each evening we experience the sunset.

Standing in the light of the setting sun, we enter a different sort of sacred space. There is a gradual shifting of tones as the light changes from the clear brightness of late afternoon through the soft, warm of evening. The sun sinks low onto the horizon, spilling its golden fingers up through the clouds in rays of glorious orange and yellow light, upwards into the empty heavens, tingeing the clouds with pink and crimson. Eventually it starts to fade, changing, with the dimming of the light. Night is on its way, the sun is dying, as it does each day.

Chanting at sunset, as we often do at our centre in France, or simply watching the red-gold globe of the sun descending to the horizon amid streams of misty cloud, leaves traces in the mind long after the light has faded. Watching it, we stand in sacred space. Transient, and yet repeating with each day's cycle, linking us to the eternal.

Such experiences seem to bridge the actual and the metaphoric. In many traditions the sunset is associated with death. The disappearing sun mirrors the seeping of life from the body, softly, slowly, but unrelentingly. As we stand watching the process of the ending of day, we see reflected back to us, rehearsed within us, our own ending. Not violent or pained, but natural and bathed in beauty. We feel at some level our capacity for a good death. Letting go of life and slipping into the inevitable, for death comes just as certainly as the sun sets, we practise our end without even realising it, breathing silently into the last breath of light as it extinguishes. Each sunset is different. Each gives us a different message.

When I have stood by the bed of a dying person in the hospital where I visit as a volunteer chaplain, chanting nembutsu, our call to the measureless, I feel that warm soft energy of the sunset enfolding me and the patient. Those precious moments, deeply beautiful in their pathos, are permeated for me by the images of fading rays and the visceral feeling of this sacred time when light slips into darkness. In feeling it, I offer it to my companion.

Sunset and dawn are sacred times, often the times of ceremonies and rituals, but more basically, rooted in our human sense of unfolding time, of birth and death and the life-giving warmth of the sun. Often they are literally the times of births and deaths. Our bones know what science tells us, our relationship with and complete dependence on the daily arrival and departure of the light.

But sacredness is more a matter of the way we approach things than of the things themselves. Being in natural surroundings provides a reminder for us to give reverent attention to all the ordinary places which we visit.

In Buddhist psychology, reverent attention, *adhimoksha*, is seen as the quality which arises from the transformation of the grasping mentality which tries to possess the things which it encounters, sweeping them into our personal psychological games rather than simply seeing them as they are. When we look with reverence, our involvement with nature becomes a spiritual practice. We look and love.

A friend of mine, Richard, compares walking in nature to the religious practice of Lectio Divina, or divine reading, a Christian practice in which the devotee reads from the Bible or another holy book, allowing the text to speak to him or her and inspire spiritual contemplation.

On occasion out and about in places such as Highgate Wood near where I live I have the distinct impression of being spoken to by the natural world, the birdsong, the wind moving through the tree. Each species of tree has its own dialect if I listen closely enough... In fact it's all amazing isn't it? To approach nature as a form of Lectio Divina, as a living book, is I think a really valid form of nembutsu, or of prayer, providing we do it reverently and mindfully. Walking barefoot on the grass; apparently Sitting Bull did this as a form of prayer each morning. It's lovely after rainfall.

For Richard, who works outdoors in environmental projects, the world of nature is the sacred space. It offers a place of devotion and spiritual inspiration which transcends particular practices, but draws together experiences expressed in Christianity, Buddhism and Native American religion. In nature he finds a route to spiritual truth in which his encounters with nature speak to him directly, offering inspiration and wisdom.

Chapter Four

Writing and Art in Other-Centred Work

This morning I wrote about the sacred space of the bamboo grove. Then this afternoon Massimo invites us to join him in the bamboo grove for meditation. It is five days since I was last there. Now Massimo is leading the bio-dance week, the next event on our summer programme.

So it is that I return to the grove. I sit in my habitual space, partly out of a feeling of nostalgia for last week and partly just because it is there, a space. It is nice to be back. The space has taken on a personal association with practice and with my connection to the natural world.

When I sit down in the bamboo and look around me, I am immediately struck by how much I did not include in my writing this morning. Indeed, I become aware that, although I felt a strong sense of the place as I was writing, the image in my mind was impressionistic and lacking in many important specific details. I have been wrapping words around my sense of the space, the memory, the sounds, and the experience of meditating outdoors. Now back in the meditation place, realising the gaps in my recall makes me look more carefully. I look into the bamboo stems, stunning in their clarity and, as I do so, I feel shocked by confronting the chasms in my memory.

Immediately I become aware, for example, that my earlier description of the bamboo omitted almost completely any mention of the way the stems are jointed. My mental image was of tall, elegant stems and a fine filter of leaves against the sky. Now I am actually looking at the canes in front of me; the joints fascinate me. Realising my omission has made me even more attentive to the details.

The characteristic segments at intervals up the canes are not uniform. On some stems they are close together, and on others they are further apart. These joints also vary in the way the affect the contours of the cane. Some are tight, like garters which are not big enough, pinching the cane so that it bulges between them, creating a profile of curves. Others are simply horizontal bars around the cane, interruptions of the vertical line that do not alter its outline at all. While most of the canes have joints which are straight, perpendicular to the stem, some have ones which lie at angles to the length, and where this happens, they alternate in direction, creating canes whose contours twist to and fro like sugar barley walking sticks.

The stems also vary considerably in thickness. Some are thin, perhaps a centimetre in diameter, like garden canes. Others are maybe twice or three times this thickness, sturdy enough to make furniture or other constructions. The colours vary too, far more than I recalled in my earlier writing, a rich palate which ranges from the bright emerald green of new, thick stems, through to the pale brown of the dry, dead ones. Between these colours are olive greens, ochres and greys. Some colours are smooth and even, whilst others are mottled, or shaded from green to brown on the same stem.

Looking round I notice other details. The leaves on which I am sitting are now damp after the earlier rain. I notice that although they are indeed elliptical as I described, they also have finely pointed tips. Some of the bamboos have side branches, but many do not, and it appears that some of these bare stems have dropped their branches to the ground leaving the canes as smooth uprights, with small protuberances where the branches used to be. I realise that I had constructed an image of these branches from those which I saw on cut canes, not taking into account that, actually, over time, those canes left in situ within the clump drop their side arms. Does this happen only to those surrounded by other canes, I wonder, or is it a general feature of aging canes? Observation evokes curiosity.

Writing about detail

Writing can be a useful way to sharpen the mind and connect with the world, but it can also dull our perception, for we all too easily get caught in words and the familiar patterns of our thinking, preventing ourselves from seeing the real things around us. We can end up elaborating stories about what we have experienced and creating justifications for our viewpoints by reiterating our prejudices and beliefs.

On solitary retreat, for example, keeping a journal can focus the attention and push us to look more deeply at our experience as we record thoughts, and then question our recording of them, but it can also take us off into long detours of imagination in which we question very little and construct a story about the experience, writing something which is only a loose approximation to the reality. Writing is a tool which can be harnessed in other-centred enquiry, but it needs to be used with a critical edge. We need to keep asking ourselves, "Is what I have written true?" and "Can I put this more succinctly, more accurately, in more detail?"

Writing takes many different forms. Some writing aims to convey facts about the world. It is concrete and pared down to provable details. But even when the writing seems to be a straightforward account of events or concepts, the factual material in the piece is not all that is conveyed. The writing also tells something about the writer's relationship to their subject. Even a scientific paper has a viewpoint. Its language and form convey an attitude to its topic. On the one hand it takes a stance of impartial observation, and on the other it is imbued with the ethos of the current scientific paradigm. All writing is like this, however much we try to take ourselves out of the picture.

My pieces of writing about the bamboo grove were attempts to describe in detail the features of the space. At the same time, they also attempted, in giving this factual information, to do so in such a way as to convey to the reader something of the experience of sitting there. This process incorporated both the intention to observe accurately and the intention to convey the feeling experience which I had whilst sitting in the bamboo grove, meditating. These elements or the space, its contents, and myself as observer were all explicitly apparent, but there was also an unseen participant in the process, the reader. Without ever being mentioned, you were present as a factor in the creation of the piece of writing.

This is typical of much writing. The writer is a bridge, a mediator of experience, passing on as eloquently as he or she is able the flavour of something to the reader, who may never have known the situation directly. In this way, the writer has two masters, two 'others' to consider and attend to. The writing forms a bridge between the original experience and the reader. The writer finds a voice in which to describe the original situation, but the reader has needs and preferences and will interpret the piece of writing through his or her own filter of thought. We could see the writer as simply the messenger, the mode of transmission, mediating experience for the reader.

All writing has an audience. The act of committing ideas to paper or computer screen creates a reader. Even when the writing is private, a jotting down of unprocessed innermost thoughts, there will be a reader. It may be the writer him or herself, returning to the notes days or years later. It may be another person, known or unknown. It may be the universe. Somewhere, though, there is an intended reader, otherwise it would not be written. Thus all writing involves another, and often it is shaped by the fantasy presence of that other, like a ghostly figure, peering over the author's shoulder, whose reactions must be anticipated.

Writing can thus be factual, descriptive, impressionistic and imaginative. It slides a scale between these modes, but is never fully one or other. When we are present in a place such as the bamboo grove, in one sense, we have a direct experience of being in a real place, but as we have already seen, even the most apparently direct experiencing is mediated. Before we have even thought of writing about it, our minds are already processing the information which our senses have grasped, putting it into words for us. Our perception is conditioned, as are our reactions.

Among these conditioned processes, language plays a significant part, for one of the ways that we mediate experience is by putting it into language. At first the language is a rough approximation. If we sit among the bamboo stems and close our eyes we probably simply think "I am sitting among the bamboo". We probably have a vague impression of stems, partly derived from what we have just seen and partly from our concept of 'bamboo canes'.

Then the intention to write about the experience forces us to look more accurately. What do bamboo canes actually look like? What colours are they? How do the leaves look against the sky? How are they spaced? The prospect of writing itself conditions a fuller examination of the bamboo as we rehearse the piece we must later put into words. We are pushed to look again.

Some of my description of the bamboo is concrete. I notice the range of forms. I can list them. I can catalogue the variety of colours, the numbers of sectional bands, and the frequency of side branches. I might even be able to identify varieties and give their Latin names if I were a bamboo expert. It all seems neutral and obvious, telling things as they are. But even in describing things in this way, the language that I choose also conveys meaning. For example, if I describe their colour as bright green, the image which the reader is likely to have will probably be different from that which would be imagined if I describe the canes as emerald green. The first choice of words perhaps evokes an image of colours in a paint box, whilst the second evokes the rich transparent colour of a gemstone. In choosing words, we hint at comparisons and contexts, offering subtle colouration to the information which we are conveying.

Sometimes, though, when we are writing we deliberately focus on conveying the aspects of the experience which are not easily categorised or documented by facts. We may, for example, write poetry. The words can paint pictures which are abstract and evocative. But once again, to write good poetry we need to look more closely at the objects or experiences which we are describing. We need to find ways to phrase our perception which are not hackneyed and stale, and doing this requires freshness of view. We thus learn to feel more attentively the fine grain of the encounter.

Poetry is a dance of detail. It invites the reader to inhabit the place, the object, the writer's viewpoint which inspires the work and to find words to describe and enhance that experience. It attempts to convey a being-ness, and to share the wordless through words, but also to build and create and play until something new emerges which is more than the original. Writing poetry has often been a part of the spiritual life, as spiritual experience and meaning is often hard to convey in direct language.

But writing can also be important in developing our awareness and sensitivity to ordinary things. It can be a helpful exercise to write a description of a place in which you have been working from memory. Try to record as much detail as possible, as accurately and colourfully as you can. Imaginatively return to the place so that you capture the specifics of what you see and feel there. Then go back to the actual place and sit and look. See how accurate your memory was and also the ways in which it distorted things. Sit for about ten minutes taking in the scene again, then go away and write some more. As you repeat this cycle several times explore how the writing process is affecting your view of the place and also how your changing view of it is affecting your writing. Notice to what degree you are seeing the place more clearly and to what degree you are refining a story about it.

Art and seeing

Just as writing can be a way to develop our capacity to see more intently, so too other forms of creative art can help us to develop a sharpness of vision. Conversely, writing can be used to reinforce the self-story and so too can art. Some art is introspective and deliberately self-expressive, but other art is an attempt to communicate an experience of the world to others.

Of course these distinctions are not clear cut, and both aspects can be seen in a great work of art. They are dimensions of the creative process which encompasses many strands of communication. Nevertheless some pieces of art are unquestionably more concerned with the artist's personal experience, whilst others attempt to relate to the world and convey it to others.

Other-centred work is concerned with developing empathy for others. In art there are a number of 'others' to which we relate. We can develop empathy for our subject, our audience and also the medium in which we are working. We can allow all three to speak to us and expand our capacity for creativity and engagement.

So if we are exploring other-centred approaches in the visual arts, not only are we mediating between the subject matter and the audience, we also have the opportunity to develop empathy for the medium itself. We can try to use our materials in ways which best draw out their potential. Whether painting or sculpture, pencil drawing or pastel, the medium in which the artist works imposes a set of conditions and also invites particular possibilities. Some media tend to demand precision, such as drawing with pencil or pen and ink, whilst others such as painting or modelling are more robust, allowing a representation to build up through a process of layering and experimentation. Media such as clay, papier mâché work, or oil paint have texture, and with them the process of creation is as much a tactile as a visual one. Exploring these possibilities we extend the range of art which we produce.

Nature itself provides materials which can be used creatively. Here there is a particular opportunity to connect with the natural world by developing empathy for the materials we use. Interesting pieces of wood, stones, sheep's wool, seed heads and even the landscape itself can all be used in making art. The artist interacts with the elements of the environment, subtly rearranging it with respect for the qualities of the materials with which he or she is working.

An artist like Andy Goldsworthy is well known for his work, which is generally created in situ out of local materials. Such works are often temporal: a pile of stones on a beach which time and tide will topple or coloured leaves arranged in a perfect circle, floating on the still water of a hollow in a stream, witnessed perhaps only by the artist himself and preserved in a photograph.[16]

In the past I have run creative workshops based in nature. In these I ask group members to go out and find objects in the natural world which speak to them. They might find a range of things: bark or leaves, feathers or stones, twigs or coloured earth. They bring these things back to the group space where they sit with them, regarding them with meditative attention and asking them how they might be used creatively. What might they become? Only after they have sat for a while like this do they start to work creatively with the materials.

This attitude of invitation can extend to more traditional media. I encourage participants in such a workshop to explore the use of different materials, like paint, pastel or pens, discovering how each of them behaves: what sorts of mark it can make, and how it works on different surfaces; what it wants to create.

The context can also create opportunities. Objects can be embedded in the earth, rooted as the stones in a Zen garden, or they can be hung from trees, in motion with wind and the movement of the branch itself. Placing them in particular relationships with one another or with the wider working area, natural attributes of the objects can be amplified and their three dimensional qualities can be explored as well as the qualities of in-between spaces which they create as they interact.

As artists work, they become more sensitive to the materials which they use, working with their strengths and drawing out their beauty. Earlier this year I met the Japanese woodworker, Miyazaki.[17] Miya lives in the hills behind Northampton, Massachusetts. He works with natural wood, often obtained locally from trees which have fallen in winter storms. On the January day that I visited him and his wife Susan, Miya was out looking at some trees which had been blown over by the wind on a neighbouring farm.

Miya's work is very fine, and meticulously finished. It blends traditional woodworking skills of cutting, jointing and polishing with a profound sensitivity to the wood itself and an eye for contemporary design. We sat around the dining table drinking coffee and he talked about his art. The table was itself a piece of Miya's work, its top was a huge slice of wood taken out of a full grown tree, smoothed and polished so that the swirls of grain showed. Miya had not chosen a straight piece of wood, for the table was irregularly shaped, with protuberances which were once the stumps of branches. There was a fissure starting at one end and running up the middle of the piece; a small uneven crack that split the surface. The wood flowed in its own shape and the table celebrated this movement. Nor was this some tacky piece of rough wood furniture, cut with the bark still on to look rustic. Miya's craftsmanship was extraordinary. He had inset wedges of contrasting wood, shaped like stylised butterflies, across the break in the surface, tying the two halves of the table together with this decorative motif, and so created a masterpiece in the original sense of the term.

The house and the workshop beneath it were full of other pieces of Miyazaki's work, some finished and others in process of production. There were elegant reclining seats, fashioned out of complete pieces of wood, sculptures of interweaving branches, and even a pair of sofas, still unfinished, made from the two hollowed out halves of a massive tree trunk. There were also handbags. Some years ago Miya's wooden handbags created quite a stir when they sold in the exclusive shops of New York and London's fashion districts.

The remainder of these latter works of art hang on the living room wall now, perfect wooden containers of all shapes and sizes, highly polished like wooden pebbles on a wet shoreline, showing the beautiful grain of the different coloured woods that he used to make them. Some of the bags have lids which are hinged. Some are rounded and others geometric with square corners and tongue and grooved joints. All show the same reverence and sensitivity for the material of which they were made, examples of a craft grounded in a deep appreciation of the natural resource.

In other-centred work, we can connect with natural materials as media which can be transformed into works of art. We can also use art as a means of communication to share our experience of the natural world. Drawing and painting from nature, we develop our capacity to observe and our appreciation of the natural phenomena which we try to represent. Art of this kind is about careful attention to detail. Just as in writing, we have to train ourselves to look more intensely at our subject and see the details which we want to describe.

Drawing and painting from nature, the artist engages with the subject with intense attention. It can be tempting to draw what one imagines the subject to look like, but the artistic process demands that we look again and again and again. Creative art is a trialogue, a conversation between artist, subject and image. The artist investigates and then expresses what he or she has seen.

Recently I visited a friend of a friend who was a landscape painter. After I had seen a variety of his work, I commented that he used a very wide range of different colours and styles in his paintings. Some of his work was vividly coloured, with bright blues of sea and sky and sharp detailing of people and buildings. Others were painted in soft, subtle colours, beiges and greys, fading into a misty haze.

He laughed. "That's the difference between a studio artist and one who paints from nature," he said. "A studio artist paints from what he imagines or remembers. He develops his own range of colours. Painting from nature, you paint it how it is, and nature is constantly changing."

Memory distorts experience. As soon as we leave a place or object, our memory stores away an image which is basically a construction. When we look at a scene, our mind interprets it and once we have left the place, the imagination has free reign to fill in the gaps of memory. So, in the privacy of the studio, the mind has the liberty to embroider memories according to its habitual blueprints. We are naturally lazy, living by approximations, so unless we question ourselves and look again at nature, we fall into our own range of standard colours.

Drawing from nature forces us to look intently. But even when we are actually looking, our preconceptions are a problem. Art teachers sometimes use tricks to get the students to really look at the objects in front of them instead of working from their assumptions about them. For example, a student may be told to draw the spaces between the branches of a tree instead of the branches themselves, or to draw a face without using any outlines, only using shading to show its light and dark planes. Such exercises train the eye and are useful to us in challenging habits of perception, as well as in creating works of art. We think we know what a tree or a face looks like but we do not have images of spaces or shadows stored away.

Working intently on a drawing is meditation. It demands intense focus. When I studied art at sixth form, I had to spend hours drawing from objects and from life. I remember that after I had been drawing intensively, on several occasions, I experienced the sort of phenomena that one associates with intensive spiritual practice. Scenes which I encountered whilst out walking would become radiantly bright. They would seem to me to be perfect, and fill me with a sense of complete contentment as I looked at them. Ordinary things would appear sharp and luminous.

I am sure that these experiences were rooted in the intensity with which I was working, as I tried to see things as they actually were so that I could draw them accurately. I was literally losing myself in my work. I never produced great art, but I did achieve that special kind of perception for some of that time.

Art and poetry in the Pureland tradition

Pureland Buddhism, in which other-centred approach is rooted, has produced a good number of poets and artists. In medieval Japan there was a tradition of wandering monks and religious ascetics, many of whom went from place to place, teaching in the villages and countryside. A number of these people wrote poetry. Their work is particularly rich in natural imagery.

Perhaps the best known poet of this tradition was the eleventh century poet monk, Saigyo.[18] Saigyo's poetry, which I have reflected on elsewhere,[19] captures the spirit of the natural world, expressing his spiritual life through imagery drawn directly from his experiences of ordinary things around him. Highly evocative, it expresses the feeling of *yugen*, the wistful longing which hangs in our hearts like autumn mist, hinting at eternal truths, which are yet veiled by the clouding of distance.

Yugen is the spiritual sense which looks out beyond the horizon of ordinary experience, whilst at the same time fully appreciating its beauty and transience. It is both aesthetic and subtle; it holds our attention, and yet still remains shrouded in mystery.

Saigyo's poetry is at once simple, expressed in a few short lines of description, carefully observed and leanly written, and complex, containing, as it does, layers of allusion and resonances. For the modern reader some associations are lost, being rooted in the traditions of medieval Japanese poetry, but the imagery still speaks to us of the layered quality of religious experience. When watching birds in flight or the sun descending in the west, reed beds in autumn or thawing ice in spring, which Saigyo describes, we can intuit spiritual truth if we look with our hearts as well as our minds.

In attempting to look deeply into our experience of nature, we discover the spiritual beauty which lies within the ordinary unfolding of the seasons and the cycles of life. In communicating the experience, we may free ourselves a little if we can move beyond jaded views and tired analogies. The search for art becomes equated with the spiritual life itself, a mirror to the spaces which we inhabit and their impact upon us, and our striving to create it becomes a practice.

Chapter Five

Structures and Spaces

Our walk this morning leads us around the site in a winding path which encompasses some of the different areas where we have worked. We begin as usual with a few minutes of grounding exercises, bringing ourselves to awareness of our presence on the earth with our minds and our bodies. Although we are physically present in the place that we are in at a given time, too often our minds are preoccupied with thoughts about things which are not connected with our surroundings, running away into planning or anxieties or dreams. In everyday life this is normal and often appropriate, but during the group time we want to practise slowing down and being more connected to our immediate environment, observing the space we pass through and how our surroundings affect us. Part of our purpose in this group is to allow the natural world to impact upon us and speak to us.

So we stand beneath the walnut tree, our daily starting point. Bringing ourselves to focused attention, we feel the physicality of the contact which our feet make with the ground. We bring to awareness our presence in the space of the yard. We observe the air, warm with the morning sun and the sounds of farm vehicles in the distance. Particularly this morning, though, we are focusing on observing structure, so we start by giving our attention to our own structured nature.

Our bodies stand. How remarkable. Although we rarely, if ever, think of it, the idea that something as large as a human being could balance for so much of its time on two small feet is quite astounding. We are very cleverly constructed creatures. Evolution has done a good job on the whole. Unlike our four-legged ancestors, we have learned to stand on our two feet, gaining the advantages of height and speed and manual dexterity. Our bodies have more or less adapted to the new orientation. We have bones and sinews and muscles which help us to walk tall. No longer so bound to the earth by gravity, we reach up into the sky through the mechanics of our construction.

So in this first grounding exercise, we summon our scattered attention. We then bring our awareness in particular to the body's structural qualities and its abilities to stand. We can think of this as an upward force, the capacity of our bodies to resist gravity and hold an upright posture. Whether sitting, standing or walking, most of the time our bodies exercise these structural capacities. Only when we lie completely relaxed upon the earth do our bodies start to give up this function, and even then, usually there is some resistance, some tension of muscles, which holds the body back from complete relaxation, pushing upward against the force of gravity.

It is good to be able to give up this resistance on occasions and let go completely, but the reality is that we need structural energy in order to function most of the time. Our capacity to use these structural processes to move and sit and stand is largely automatic. We do not think, 'I will lift my foot, I will hold my spine erect, I will raise my arm.' We just do it. In being alive, we use our body structure.

Outside the body, structure exists in relationship to space. It gives form to the fluidity of empty expanses, breaking up the nothingness with features. It creates boundaries which contain the different areas of unlabelled space and defines them into fields or rooms or gardens. Space flows into the crevices between structures, the openings left by the gaps between objects. When we lift an arm we move it through space, creating new forms and new interruptions of the three-dimensional territory which we inhabit. So, in our reflections, we turn our awareness to space, observing how intimately it relates to the structures of our bodies. We stand in a space. We live in spaces. Our bodies contain space.

Our initial grounding exercise has brought our attention to the body's structure in particular, but structures are everywhere, the forms which shape and define the environment through which we walk. An obvious structure nearby is the walnut tree which bends its old, split trunk in an arc, supporting the trailing branches. It cuts off our assembling place from the field, defining the edges of the space we call the lawn. Other structures around the yard have been created by humans: the old stone buildings, drystone walls, a chicken wire fence. They cut the space with straighter lines, solid demarcations which divide the territory.

Between these structures, spaces are created and delineated by those structures which surround them. The yard would not be a yard if it were not for its position between the house, the barn and meditation hall. The space in which we assemble is framed on the one side by the walnut, on another by a row of fruit trees and a wall and on the third by buildings. Each framing offers its own flavour to the space which it encloses. Some edges are clear, marked out by fences or walls; others less so, blending into one another with changes of vegetation or usage. Trees offer soft, shady edges. Buildings are sharper, harder, less yielding to natural processes of growth and change. The hedges on our fields have gradually encroached on the open ground over the years, stealing land from the field. Drystone walls collapse, leaving impromptu paths with avenues of hazel growing on either side. Buildings do not evolve and change in quite the same way, unless seriously neglected.

As we move through spaces our bodies echo their qualities. We respond to the hard edges and sharp corners of brick walls through the wariness with which we walk around them. We feel the impact of narrowness as our bodies automatically squeeze smaller to fit through tight spaces. We expand into sunny, open areas, feeling our shoulders relax, our ribs release. We shrink as we approach enclosed structures, ducking our heads well below a low slung lintel. We relax in wide spaces of field that are open to the sky. These different spaces impact not just visually but at a visceral level too. As we move through the world, we feel cramped or enabled, held or exposed by its physicality. At a subtle level which we normally do not notice, we make our way through the environment, our bodies anticipating different sorts of structures as if in an obstacle course.

Of course other factors impact on us. The things we see, their associations in our stories, levels of light and temperature all colour our responses. Today, however, we will try to detach from these other stories, at least initially, and explore the impact of the physicality of structures and spaces which we encounter upon our body sense. So, as we set out to walk, we invite the group to be aware of structure and space.

"As we walk," I suggest, "be aware of the experience of structure and space. Notice when we go through narrow spaces, or wide ones; open areas, or closed ones. Notice what sorts of structures we pass, and how they impact on you at a bodily level. What is it like walking through a narrow tunnel of trees or across an open field? How do you feel it with your body-sense?"

The walk, which takes us through many different terrains, gives opportunities to observe these bodily reactions and notice the effects of different spaces upon us. So we walk out of the yard and along the path between the garden and the field.

The garden is divided into boat-shaped raised beds which Johan created earlier in the year. These are now overflowing with vegetables. The big, lobed leaves of courgette plants tumble over the path. Against the stems nestle the first courgettes, like large green caterpillars, sleek and flecked with darker areas. They are just starting their relentless production cycle. Bean plants hang on cane tripods, leafy masses, reaching now to the tops of their strings. Cabbages are just starting to heart-up, and the leeks with their sweeping grey-green leaves and thickening stems stand tall and solid, guarding the edges of the beds from insect invaders.

The garden is ordered and easily traversed by a network of cardboard lined furrows between the vegetable beds, though these are slightly narrow, requiring some care when placing the feet. The field on the other hand is chaotic and uninviting, a tangle of grass and bramble, with thistle heads blowing fluffy down across the wild expanse. The path between the garden and the field is grassy and wide enough for us to walk more comfortably. Above the height of the grasses and most of the vegetables, the space feels open, plants reaching little beyond knee height on either side. We pass between them in single file.

Below the garden is a corner of the field which has aspirations to being a lawn. It is not quite as unruly as the open field beyond, but nevertheless is far less disciplined than the garden. The undergrowth is closing in. Now the grass is long and has not been cut this year, so seed heads wave on yellowed stems. Our path has deteriorated, now a mere parting in the vegetation. Among the grasses, small shrubs, which seem to be a sort of herbaceous elder, but defy identification, grow, and brambles invade from the patch that edges the field. Amongst this cacophony of plant life, the outlying bamboo canes of the expanding clump poke through determinedly. Once they become established, both elder and brambles will disappear.

The path meanders on between the stems of the bamboo grove. It becomes easier to follow now, carpeted with dry leaves which glide under foot as we walk. Here one is aware of uprights. The vertical stems are straight, soaring up above our heads, and surmounted by the canopy of living leaves. Morning sun filtering between the canes throws their clean, smooth edges into contrasting lines of dark and light. Although they grow densely packed, forming a tight clump, there are interesting spaces between them and, as one looks into the mass of canes, a receding pattern of differently sized stems and in-between spaces creates an intriguing feeling of depth. Other members of the group can be seen further back along the path, strung out in a line, partly obscured by the screens of canes, but still visible, snaking back towards the garden. There is separation and yet intimacy.

Leaving the bamboo, we cross a small ditch which runs down from the garden to the next field, part of a water system that was never finished. We pass beneath the power lines, three cables supported on concrete posts which sweep in parallel perspective down the hill towards the village. This feels like a transitionary space, a place that must be crossed in order to continue and yet one which does not quite include itself in our path. Its concerns are elsewhere. The lines and the ditch cut our way. Their direction is different from ours. They interrupt our route and, in the case of the ditch, need to be stepped across, but they are not of our space. They hurry us on, urging us not to dally beneath the cables or on the uneven stones which line the channel.

The path now enters a long stretch between thorn bushes and trees. This path once followed the inside edge of the field inside the hedge but as invading blackthorn and hawthorn have been allowed to grow tall, it has now become a narrow leafy channel, lined by thorn scrub, taller than any of us and in some places arching up into a tunnel. Here the foliage and twigs are tight and twisted, creating a barrier so dense that we cannot see into it. Spiders have built webs between the branches, which sometimes criss-cross the path, leaving strands of sticky gossamer on the faces and clothes of those walking at the front of the line. This space is enclosed, dark and hidden. For some it feels safe and held, whilst for others the bushes crowd in oppressively.

Cutting into a wooded field boundary, the larger trees offer a sturdier presence, they arch over the path, their canopies joining to shade the whole area. The way is now easy to follow, a trail of dark, well walked leaf mould. Large stones edge the track, remnants of an old wall which has long since disappeared. The tree trunks here are thick, though not of great age or size. Their bark is deeply scored. They are mostly oaks and maple, but one is a walnut, its grey trunk contrastingly with the other ones, being smooth and evenly coloured. Although there are places where walking is complicated by the ridges of the old walls, here the path feels established, sure of its identity.

Beside the path, the underbrush has died away, as happens in mature woodlands. Here there is evidently the possibility for exploration as the space under trees is quite easily accessed. The main path is clear and easy to follow. We feel solid walking on it, sure of our way and able to move with confidence.

Entering the next field, the path once more twists and turns between new, young trees and bushes. Here at times the edges feel constrained by brambles and blackthorn saplings, but unlike the thorn thicket, the trees here are mostly small oaks and maples, green and fresh, with broad leaves that filter sunlight and are soft to touch. It is a lively, interesting area, bursting with its youth, for this collection of trees has grown up in the last twenty years since we have owned the land. Each turn of the path brings more surprises: a wild pear with small hard fruit growing on it, old man's beard with its white, wiry flowers and wispy tendrils tumbling over a bush, an ants' nest, a knee high mound of red clay built between the grasses. There are small clearings filled with flowers, interesting parcels of land, like forgotten cottage gardens, and patches of brambles whose leaves are turning red through the effects of poor soil and not much rain. This space feels edgy and unpredictable, light and enjoyable, but also disorientating and chaotic as paths fork and turn and back up on themselves. It is easy to lose direction here, and in it my body feels like a young colt, frisky and nervous.

Crossing a further hedge, we enter the field in which we

made our working space the previous day. The cleared area which we call the dance circle is at the lower edge of this grassy field. It is nestled into the lee of the hillside and feels safe and held by the bank behind it. Two huge oak trees grow at the lowest edge of this field. Bulbous headed where they were cut in the past, as oaks in these parts were, to create low growing branches for cattle fodder, they are called tadpole oaks, or, in French, chênes en têtard. Last year's fallen leaves still coat the ground beneath them in a smooth layer of leaf mould. It is soft and sumptuous underfoot. There is a feeling of homecoming.

The group have commented before on the atmosphere in this field. It is particularly attractive because of its steep slopes and the way it curves around the hill. The field is enclosed on all sides by good sized trees, but is, itself, relatively open, giving an impression of enclosure and comfort without oppressiveness. The sloping bank is covered with long grass and meadow flowers. It feels timeless, being much the same as it must have been for centuries. I love watching people arriving in the dance area. They come down the hillside by the path, figures passing through a landscape of waving grass stems and scabious flowers.

We leave this haven, climbing the slope by the continuing stretch of path that ascends the hill, cutting across the centre of the field. At the top is the wood which extends along the ridge on which the house is built. This wood is edged by larger trees, but behind these is a patch of younger woodland. The bramble has recently died out from beneath the trees, its last straggly remnants having disappeared only a couple of years ago. The trees are still small. They are interesting, curving shapes, with many low branches and twisted trunks, probably as a result of being eaten by deer in their early years when they stood in open field. More recently they have thrived as the deer would have been kept out by the undergrowth of bramble. Only once they reached sufficient height to shade the area did the bramble disappear. By then, of course, they were too big to be destroyed by foraging deer. Thus one of nature's cycles of natural defences completed its role.

We leave the path and scramble through the open space among the junior oaks and maples, ducking between angled trunks and avoiding overhanging vines and blackberry trailers. It is difficult walking, and with no path, we move quickly and awkwardly as if hurrying through hostile territory. No longer in line, the group is scattered between the trees, finding individual tracks across the wood. It is not a comfortable space despite its openness, and the discomfort propels us on.

Beyond this young wood, we enter a more established area of the woodland. Several large oaks, also en têtard, dominate the space. Their branches grow high into a leafy roof out of the swollen tops of their shortened trunks. Smaller hawthorn and elder are scattered across the areas between these giants. This is our destination.

In the middle of the wood we find the clearing. It is elliptical, edged by trees on three sides, and with the remnants of a wooden structure on the fourth. This structure consists of four corner posts with cross pieces bolted between them, standing eight or ten feet tall, but leaning at an angle, propped against a tree where it has fallen. These are old oak roof timbers, side struts salvaged from the meditation hall roof when it was replaced some years ago. A volunteer who stayed with us one summer a while back began to build a hut here, but the frame was never finished and a storm has bent it sideways. Perhaps someone will continue the project one day. Meantime it hovers, a wrecked ship in the forest, evocative of abandoned places and half-dreamed plans.

The floor of the clearing is overgrown with a light carpet of green. Ground hugging plants have invaded this space, which in past years has served as a meeting space. The dead heads of bluebells and Star of Bethlehem, bleached white, their seed pods burst open, stand proud among the leaves. We form a circle, standing between the tall trees, our silent walk of exploration complete.

"We are going to work in this space today," Sundari invites the group. "Take some time to explore it. Get a feel for its qualities. Take yourself into the spaces between the objects that you find around you: the trees, the stones, the things that humans have put here. Feel the energies of the different spaces, the body sense they evoke. Get to know the structures. See how they impact on you bodily. Relate to them in a physical way. See what they invite you to do, how they invite you to be. Play and interact with them."

The group scatters. People move in all directions, some near, some far. One person squeezes between the smooth bowls of three trees which are growing close together, twisting his body, serpentine, into the wooden cleft. Another explores the mossy remains of walls, tumbling lines of limestone plates which once marked field boundaries, or perhaps the collapsed remains of a cottage.

Someone else discovers a rope, hung and knotted from one of the big oaks, access to the high platform where the enlarged head splits into numerous branches, a seat, a vantage point, some fifteen feet above the ground, where one might sit and survey the forest and the world beyond. With a scuffle of boot soles on the bark, he clambers up. With childlike enthusiasm, he abandons himself to the arms of the tree. Others explore the undergrowth, or walk slowly and meditatively between the trunks, moving from the open space of the clearing into the more confused spaces of the smaller trees and back again. One person leaves the wood and walks in the sunlight on the cut swathe of the electricity line which runs adjacent to it.

Wide spaces, narrow spaces, twisted spaces, tall spaces, open or closed, light or dark, each leaves its shadow on the body as our feeling response is evoked. As we pass through them, we react. So in this exploration, we observe these reactions, conditioned by our pasts, our associations and our animal nature. So we reconvene our circle in the clearing. Sitting on the soft foliage that clothes it, we take some time to share our perceptions.

Work of this kind functions on many levels. It is a dance, a conversation, between group leader, group and nature. The steps are not predetermined, although there is a repertoire of possibilities on which we can draw. Like so much of life, the process is held in the tension between the conditioned paths of past activities and old thought processes, and the new responses, evoked by the fresh encounter with previously unknown spaces.

One cannot predict which of the many strands will surface as predominant in a group. The whole process is like a symphony with many instruments playing different melodies and counterpoints. Some themes lurk like bass tones, unobtrusive but necessary to the depth and complexity of the whole. Others rise and die like brief solos against the general background flow of the movement. Yet others blend into the melody, comfortably merging with greater themes. As facilitator and therapist, one can feel a bit like an orchestral conductor, holding each voice in the ensemble and guarding the integrity of the whole process, whilst drawing out particular aspect for emphasis.

In this morning's work the initial grounding and embodiment exercise serves rather as playing scales does for the musician. It is an opportunity to tune in and to hone the skills of bodily observation. In addition, though, it introduces a second level of body scanning. We have in the past worked with grounding, but today, the main focus of attention is drawn towards the upward force of the body itself, the structuring which holds us upright and supports our movements.

About twenty years ago, when such things were at their peak,

David and I were invited to run a weekend of personal growth in Liverpool. We asked the woman who had invited us what she would like us to do.

"Oh, it's Liverpool, something wacky!" she responded, jocularly.

So it was that in the same spirit of jocularity, we sent her a proposal for a course on Wa-Ki, 'an ancient form of body therapy'. Somehow the joke got advertised, and people started to book for the weekend. Thus it was that I suddenly found myself with the task of thinking what Wa-Ki might actually look like. I had always had in mind to run a weekend of body-work, drawing on my experience in various body focused traditions, so I decided to put together a form which expressed the core of what I did. Naming a new therapy seemed to demand a structure so I created one. Thus Wa-Ki was born.

What emerged was a simple system of awareness which I still use as a basic guide to facilitate body awareness exercises with groups. It is interesting how naming a procedure gives structure and structure in turn enables creative integration. The model which resulted consisted of four levels of body exploration. It was not so different from many systems, but was original in its particulars. I find it a useful way to think about our body process when I am leading awareness exercises.

The first level of Wa-Ki was grounding. This basic first step is common to most systems of bodywork. It involves recognising and strengthening our connection to the earth. Our downward energy roots us to the greater whole and we can enhance this sense of connection by visualising our roots descending into the soil beneath us. I have already described grounding exercises at some length in the first chapter of this book.

The second level in the model involved the exploration of structure. This focused on the upward force within the body. Skeleton and muscles hold us upright as we walk, stand or sit.

Structural energy provides the strength which creates posture. We work with structure when we stretch upwards, or expand our rib cages by reaching out our arms. We extend the spine and shoulders, maybe imagining a line rising from the crown of the head to the ceiling or sky. We stand, consciously, holding our head and back aligned.

Thus in Wa-Ki, these two tensions, the downward and the upward, are seen as holding the body in a kind of equilibrium. If we intentionally bring our awareness to them, we can feel a healthy stretch between the two opposing forces. Our structural energy draws us upward, whilst our groundedness helps us to relax and engage in a downward direction. If we let these energies grow weak, we become slouched and flaccid. If they are strong, we feel energised, and ready for action.

The further two levels of the Wa-Ki model involved work with outward and inward connections. Using the breath, it firstly connects to the surrounding space of the environment, and then to the inner space of the body. The first of these connections, to the outward experience, is characterised primarily in the breathing. Our breath reaches into space, away from the body and into the environment in which the body stands. This outward energy creates connection, it touches otherness. The body naturally relaxes into contact with its world. We complete the connection with the in-breath, drawing in the richness of our surroundings, before breathing out again and reaching further into the space which surrounds us. This outward awareness is held for several cycles of breath.

The final level of Wa-Ki involved focusing on the inward direction. With this step, we delve with our attention deep into the central body space, drawing the breath and the awareness into the belly area where emotional residues are often held, releasing tensions and letting go of whatever we find hidden there on the following out-breath. Through the focus of breathing, respectful attention is given to the body's defensive tensions as they are explored and then released with the outgoing breath.

One can see the process which these four steps describe as consisting of two pairs of exercises, each offering different focuses for body observation. The first pair, grounding and structure create the framework for investigation. They bring the attention into the body sense. The second pair then allows the practitioner to explore inner and outer connection using the breath, a powerful tool for exploring and releasing emotional tensions. This simple system of body-scanning has proved useful through the years and for all I know the good people of Liverpool still practise Wa-Ki.

The impact of different spaces upon each of us varies, but yet there can be common themes. For example, many people are affected by the wide open spaces of fen country. The flat horizon and large expanse of sky have strong impact upon the emotions. For a large section of the population such country is calming, reflective, maybe a little melancholic, but for another equally large population it is dull, boring and featureless. Both sets of experiences are common to enough people that one cannot say they are entirely personal, and yet at the same time they are far from universal. Even the same person may, on different days, experience the same scene in different ways.

We live amongst structures and these structures define the spaces within which we operate. A world without structures would be a world of mists and waters, featureless and undifferentiated. Trees and buildings and paths and telegraph posts all create boundaries and divisions, features and focuses which define the edges between spaces. Inhabiting the world, we are drawn into the effects of these in conditioning our emotions and our thinking. Some lands breed artists and others poets, some fighters, and others intellectuals. Who knows how much such trends are influenced by the ground itself on which they live and die.

Chapter Six

Boundary and Therapeutic Space

The walnut tree becomes our home. Each morning when we start our group we assemble in its shade. We stand in a circle. As group members appear out of the building or from across the yard, they join us, silently, without the need to be called. They stand, feet planted comfortably on the ground, already starting the grounding exercise before ever the first instruction is given.

It is to this place that we return at the end of the session. We walk back together from wherever we have been working, generally in silence, generally with attention on our surroundings. Often we take a different route from that by which we went out. Thus we circle the site: one way out, another way back.

We do not necessarily talk on our return. Silent assembly is enough to give acknowledgement and closure to our shared work. Sometimes we simply agree the next meeting time. We touch base. The walnut tree is our space. A working area, here we wash our clothes, relax, eat our meals. It is a safe place, a comfortable place. It is the group home.

Therapeutic boundaries

Therapeutic space is boundaried. A boundary is a structure which enables a space to exist. The therapeutic boundary has a number of dimensions. It is psychological, social and physical. It creates both safety and intensity. By setting limits in some respects, it gives permission in others. It creates clarity about what is and what is not included in the therapeutic relationship and it protects the therapeutic space from intrusion of outside influences. This makes it possible for the client to let go of some of the defences which he or she might hold onto in daily life and to become more vulnerable. The therapeutic boundary creates intensity but it also creates a sense of coming home within the therapy room. It helps the client to feel protected enough to let go of some layers of psychological armouring.

In conventional therapies, the therapeutic boundary is most obviously held by the physical space of the consulting room. The fact that the room is private, has a closed door and is not overlooked, provides one dimension of the safety which is necessary to the therapeutic process. There may be other physical features which convey this sense of safe space: the way the room is furnished and decorated, the presence of materials for use in therapeutic activities and an absence of more personal artefacts belonging to the therapist. These latter aspects will be more specific to the particular therapist and their model. For example some therapists may be more keen to make the room anonymous than others. Some will have paints and other creative media, others not.

Time is also an important boundary which gives the session structure. Although the strictness of timekeeping varies between models, most therapists work to fixed length sessions and offer pre-planned appointments.

Other therapeutic boundaries are less visible but none the less are vital. Mostly these depend upon the therapist's behaviour. The therapist will probably not be personally revealing, except in as much as things shared have direct and obvious relevance for the client. Social chat will be avoided, and if it occurs, will be regarded as part of the therapeutic material to be reflected on. Whatever is said between therapist and client may be openly discussed in terms of what it reveals about the client's personal patterns and experience. Therapists will not see their clients outside therapy sessions or socialise with them. Thus the relationship, though it may be warm and even loving, will remain professional and not cross the line into friendship or romance. Primarily it will be a one-way relationship. The therapist's responsibility is to create therapeutic space for the client, and not the reverse, however inviting the client may be. The purpose is to benefit the client, and in order to support this, the therapist will deal with any of his or her own personal needs that arise in the course of their therapeutic work elsewhere by taking them to supervision or to personal therapy.

Therapeutic work in groups generally maintains similar boundaries to individual therapy, and group therapists also aim to establish a safe, private environment, with ground-rules and clear time boundaries. This, again, offers structure to the sessions. As in one to one therapy, the facilitators are unlikely to be self-revealing and will tend to regard unexpected thoughts and feelings which they have whilst facilitating the group as part of the group process. These may be reflected on in the context of what they say about the group, if they are shared at all, but the facilitators will not generally share extraneous facts about themselves. This said, styles of groupwork are more varied than those of individual work. Some therapeutic groupwork has more in common with other sorts of community based activities in which boundaries can be more fluid.

Outdoor work is commonly done in groups, though it can be done individually. In this respect, it may be compared with other group and individual therapies. Boundary issues and the limits of acceptable personal behaviour on the part of the therapist who is leading this work need to be reflected on just as they would be in regular therapy settings.

When we work out of doors, many of the considerations regarding therapeutic boundaries remain the same, but some of the factors which are considered important in conventional therapy settings are necessarily different. The environment in which the work takes place is de facto less predictable than an indoor therapy room and some factors which would be controlled in conventional therapies may not be so whilst working out of doors. This challenges the therapist to adapt, thinking through the implications in the particular circumstances of the therapeutic process. In this chapter we will review some of the issues which may arise in establishing and maintaining a therapeutic relationship in this area of work.

Therapeutic Space

The first function of the therapeutic boundary is to define the therapeutic space. The boundary clarifies the point at which the client moves from the ordinary, everyday world into the space in which therapeutic activity happens. It creates a place of safety, where experiences can become vivid and perception altered. Such experiences may ordinarily be avoided because the person needs to preserve wariness and personal defences. So the boundary is a protective structure, reverential and enabling, a magic circle, and a sacred space.

The boundary creates a gateway, a threshold. Beyond this threshold, the ordinary things of life are viewed in a different way so that they become extraordinary. Everything that occurs in this space may become the subject of scrutiny. The therapist-client relationship becomes an alliance, as the two engage in observation and reflection into the client's life-world, but the relationship can also itself become the focus of enquiry.

Events which happen around the boundary of the therapy session are often the subject of particular scrutiny. The client is seen as enacting habitual patterns of behaviour in their reaction to the artificial restriction which the time limit imposes. Therapists will commonly address incidents which occur outside the session itself by enquiring into their meaning as psychological processes. Thus the therapist will not ignore the client's throw-away comment made on the doorstep after the session has ended. It may well reveal important aspects of the client's issue. Such material is thus incorporated into the therapeutic process although, strictly speaking, it is off-limits. The fact that it is spoken in this in-between space is often an indication that the client is sharing something risky, in what he or she sees as a sort of therapeutic 'no man's land', relying on the ambiguity of the space to say things which is difficult to express in the sharper scrutiny of the therapy hour. It is therefore in some respects a breach of boundaries on the part of the therapist to re-introduce the material into the session, but at the same time an act which is important to the therapeutic process.

In this way, even in conventional therapies, boundaries are broken in order to further the therapeutic outcome. The therapist does not cease to be the therapist when the client phones up out of hours on a thin pretext. The client may have all sorts of motivations toward the therapist in behaving this way: neediness, craving for more attention or a special relationship, or a desire to disturb and punish. Raising these possibilities is important to the therapeutic process, and the therapist will consider ways of drawing the incident back into the dialogue which honour the therapeutic boundary as far as is possible. Commonly he or she will respond to such situations along the lines of, "Let's talk about this next session." Even this response traverses the line between session and ordinary life, but it avoids becoming engaged in therapeutic discourse outside the therapy hour.

Boundary issues like this become even more complex in outdoor settings. In conventional settings therapy begins on entry to the therapist's room at the start of the session and ends when the time is finished and the room is left. Working out of doors, boundaries of time and space are generally defined by some sort of explicit agreement, but they may need to be more flexible than those used in indoor work.

In outdoor work the working space is larger and probably has less clearly defined edges. The group may move through the countryside on a hike or settle in different locations for different activities. The therapists and group participants may not even necessarily be able to see one another all the time. Thus the area in which a group works may change as a session progresses or may vary from session to session. There may be spaces within spaces, places where the group assembles for a particular piece of work and then moves on.

Because this mobility can sometimes create a feeling of homelessness, some groups find it helpful to establish a base from which to go forth, a starting point to which they can return at the conclusion of the session. This space is the group home.

Establishing a home base in outdoor work

In environmentally based groupwork, the group generally begins by coming together in a defined therapeutic space. This space may be a natural space out of doors or it may be indoors. If this space is well established, it can become a space to which the group can return at the ends of sessions to reflect upon their work. As such, it becomes the group home. Whether an indoor or outdoor place is chosen for this purpose, the home space provides a place of containment for the group. It allows it to establish itself and reflect on its process without threat of inter-ruption or dispersal in the wider surroundings.

The group will usually use some of its initial meeting to establish some norms of working and ground-rules which will give further containment. These may be explicit or implicit. For example, it can be important to gain commitment from members to attending the whole of all the group sessions so that any interpersonal material can be worked through. In some contexts, in outdoor groups, members may be inclined to drift off before the end of sessions unless they have understood the importance of the debriefing process.

Such agreement supports intensity in the group, and is usually an essential aspect of the group process, but it is not necessarily the only way to work. In some settings it may be hard to achieve such a group contract, so facilitators may need to negotiate acceptable compromises. Having worked in many different circumstances and different cultures over the years, I have come to appreciate that in practice so long as the arrangement is clear to all those involved, it is possible to work in many different ways. Groups with looser boundaries can still do good work.

Commonly, then, a group creates its protected space or 'home', whether in a group room or out of doors, as a base from which it can go forth into nature, and to which it can return for the last part of the session to process and share what has been learned. This model is a good one, particularly for less experienced groups, since it creates a safe working space which is away from the places being visited. The space is thus uncontaminated by any unpleasant feelings which might be encountered in the outdoors. It gives distance from anything which may have provoked anxiety. It gives closure at the end of each session.

This is not the only way to work though. The home space need not always be returned to at the end of the session and in some cases a long debriefing after every session would take up too much group time and introduce too much talking. Even so, a regular starting and finishing place is still valuable. It creates a clear division between ordinary life and group time. It allows the session to begin with a grounding or focusing exercise and lets the facilitators set the tone for the walk to the place where the group will be working for the remainder of the session. Returning to the same spot at the end gives closure at the end.

Without an initial grounding exercise, the walk to the working place can become a social activity, with people chatting to one another along the way rather than focusing on what they are seeing and experiencing. Of course in some settings, with some groups, chatting whilst walking together may be appropriate and beneficial, for example with groups of people whose social skills are poor, or where the group will later explore its own process as part of the reflection, but with most groups chatting lowers the level of awareness and creates a missed opportunity.

Using the same spot as a home base on each session provides the group with both a sense of security and an indicator that the session has begun. The formal start becomes a sort of ritual, marking the point at which the ordinary world is exchanged for the therapeutic space. This provides a sense of continuity and gives the group identity. At the end of the session it provides a feeling of closure.

Working Spaces

Some groups will remain within a relatively small geographical area throughout their working time. They might work in a garden, park or piece of wasteland in a city. A compact space of this kind offers a feeling of containment, and, although the group may have a particular corner within such a space which they use as a home base, the space as a whole can be regarded as the group's territory.

Other groups roam more widely and are not located in one place. A group hiking across moors or climbing in mountains carries its sense of group space with it. Like a troop of monkeys or herd of deer, it moves as a body, with members staying within sight and earshot of one another most of the time, unless specific exercises dictate otherwise. Such groups still create defined areas for particular tasks, however, and, if they use exercises which involve the group splitting up, they will almost certainly establish a working boundary and beginning and end points. The facilitators will probably include spatial limits in their instructions and a reference point to which group members can return if they encounter difficulties.

In our centre in France we have thirty acres of land, which consists of fields, thicket, woods and paths. Whilst most of our work remains within this area, it is far too big for group members to use the whole space all of the time. In practice different activities require different space boundaries. Some activities are better done in smaller spaces where shouted instructions can be heard by everyone or where the whole group can interact and work together on a guided task or exercise. Other activities have wider boundaries. It can be important to give people the experience of solitariness in nature.

Time boundaries

Whilst groups involved in therapeutic activities in nature usually work to some form of time boundaries in the same way as any other group, the practicalities of the situation can mean that greater flexibility is required. Sometimes the planned finishing time may need to be open-ended. For example, where an activity involves a longer walk, it is difficult to predict how fast members will cover the distance. Also, when the group is scattered doing individual work, some members may get so absorbed in the work that they fail to return to base on time and others are left waiting. In other activities, the time required for a particular activity may be more predictable.

Group time may or may not include the time getting to the working space. Where it does, people may vary in their speed of walking, affecting the time of arriving back at base. To some extent this can be absorbed if there is a period of debriefing on return in the group 'home'.

The speed of walking is, of course, something which can be discussed along with other aspects of group process. Getting back late may indicate a group's enthusiasm for being out of doors or conversely its reluctance to engage in the final sharing circle. Arriving back late may also, however, reflect the quality of focus in the group, since a group that is more grounded and meditative will often walk more slowly. Noticing how a group walks will provide feedback to the facilitators on its mood and level of attention and this may inform their plans for future activities, even if it is not directly discussed.

At a practical level, being flexible about time boundaries is not necessarily a problem so long as the expectation is shared. When the group is hiking, for example, everyone shares some responsibility for the pace and can see if things are running behind time, so not keeping to strict time boundaries is not generally an issue for the group unless the original plan was evidently unrealistic. If a group is running behind time, it is useful to reflect on whether an element in the delay has psychological rather than practical origins, but in many cases it will be, at least in part, circumstantial factors which have caused it. Outdoor work is often based on shared responsibility and co-operative effort to a far greater extent than indoor therapeutic work.

Even where a time boundary is agreed, with outdoor work unforeseen circumstances can disrupt things, so group members need to be prepared for unpredictable finishing times. If a group member is injured or unable to keep up, for example, concerns for their safety and the need to stay together as a group will probably override the need to get back to base for a certain time.

Some exercises in the field rely upon group members timing themselves. Where group members engage in solitary work over a wide geographical area, it may not be possible to indicate the end of a session to them audibly, though the sound of whistles or gongs can carry a long way in open country. Checking that members have watches and that these are co-ordinated may help to ensure that the group does not become too widely scattered and that people return at approximately the same time, but inevitably reassembling a group after such an exercise will take some minutes.

In conclusion, participants need to be prepared to be flexible and to share some responsibility for time boundaries. If they have commitments which require them to return by a fixed time, such as collecting children from school, this needs to be allowed for in the planning process.

Residential and non-residential groups

Some groups which do environmental work are residential and some are not. Residential groups offer scope for many activities which are not possible in non-residential groups. For example, in a residential group, evening and night-time activities become possible. People can stay up through the night or sleep out in wild spaces, camping, or in the open without tents. The lengths of sessions can be varied to accommodate different sorts of activities, for example a week-long programme might well include one full day exercise alongside shorter ones on other days. The whole residential might build towards a particular activity such as a solitary activity based on the idea of a vision quest, an expedition, or a bigger group challenge. These sorts of intensive activity are much better done in circumstances where people are not returning to their daily life in between sessions, partly because the residential format allows for extended working periods and partly because it provides therapeutic holding through the follow-up time and debriefing process.

In residential settings, there is often some flexibility and ambiguity about what is considered group time. It is probably better to think of the whole period of a residential from the first morning to the last afternoon as group time, but to then work within it with different degrees of focus. In this way actual group sharing sessions would be tightly boundaried, as would some exercises, whilst other activities would be more open-ended. Things like sleeping out under the stars or cooking on a campfire might be more social and not have firm beginning and end points but they could also be intensive learning experiences for some members. There would usually be some 'downtime' scheduled within the residential, but things which occur in this time might then be raised in group sharing sessions.

In residential groups there are often dilemmas about how to

handle 'downtime'. If there is too much 'time off' a group may lose intensity or members may talk about issues arising from the group process in informal ways so that important aspects of the work are dissipated and never brought to the facilitated sessions where they can be worked through. On the other hand, if there are no gaps in the schedule the whole process can become too intense.

Facilitators may choose to control the process in various ways, for example by asking for silence after the evening session or first thing in the morning. The group may develop ground-rules about what should be talked about between sessions and conversely what gossip or chat should be reported back to the group at large. It can be helpful to think of the group process itself as a sort of environment in which there are a variety of terrains with different qualities and intensities: some thickets, some woods, some open fields, some lakes to relax by.

Interpersonal boundaries are also likely to be different where facilitators and participants are living together, whether the group is held in an outdoor activities centre or camping. Unless the facilitators keep themselves separate from the group during the downtime, they will inevitably socialise with them. Indeed, as has been suggested, the socialising will often be an integral part of the programme. Either option will have consequences.

If the facilitators stay separate they will probably be perceived as rather aloof. If they join in, they will be perceived as closer to being group members and may end up sharing more of their personal lives with the group participants. This is not a problem usually, so long as the facilitators have an awareness of their own boundaries and do not share things with the group which are too personal and likely to have negative impact on group members, or behave in inappropriate ways. In this context it would be very unwise for facilitators to consume alcohol even if participants are allowed to. In general alcohol is best avoided on residential groups.

Relationship Boundaries

It is not only in residential groups that the facilitators of environmental work may find that they are sharing more personally with group members than they would normally do with therapy clients. Working with natural environments can throw up all sorts of circumstances which alter the form of the therapeutic alliance. For the inexperienced therapist there are pitfalls in this. If a facilitator does not have good personal boundaries, or is working with particularly difficult client groups, it is easy to find problems arising from over-familiarity with group members. This means that it is worth thinking through circumstances which may cause boundary complications in advance. Despite possible concerns, the change of conventional boundaries which one experiences in environmental therapies is one of the strengths of the work.

In other-centred therapy, the ideal therapeutic relationship is triangular. Therapist and client, or facilitator and group member, together establish an alliance in order to explore an 'other'. This creates a therapeutic triangle in which the working alliance is based on establishing *fellow feeling* between therapist and client and focusing shared curiosity on enquiring into the third element, an object in the client's world.

In the case of environmental work, aspects of the natural world create the third element in this triangular relationship. It is in the shared exploration of this natural resource that change and healing takes place. Other-centred therapeutic relationships are characterised by a co-creative style of working in which both parties function in an 'adult' mode of discourse. To a greater extent they avoid becoming hooked into the more regressive, transference based relationship which is found in some other models of therapy.

Working with the environment can be physically challenging and there can be a much greater need for groups to work together, not just in order to support each other psychologically, but also to achieve physical aims. In this physical aspect the facilitator may be just as vulnerable as other group members.

Although in principle the group leaders should always work well within their physical capacities so that they are unlikely to succumb to fatigue and have sufficient reserves of energy to deal with emergency situations if they arise, it is possible for them to be taken unawares. Accidents happen and if a leader becomes sick or injured, they may be reliant upon the group for practical support. Whilst, to some extent, the presence of a co-facilitator guards the group participants against being required to take full responsibility in such circumstances, the group cannot be shielded from concern about unexpected problems that arise and still plays a mutually caring role with its facilitators.

Even without such eventualities, there is a good deal of physical intimacy in facing outdoor challenges. Dealing with bodily functions, fatigue and uncertainties of weather or terrain can bring people close and create bonds which cement the group at many levels. As facilitators are part of this process, they too may find that their relationship to group members becomes closer and more 'real' than they would in some therapies where the therapist is relatively insulated from personal challenge.

One to one work
So far, discussion of therapeutic space has mostly focused on group situations. One to one therapy in the outdoors is far less common, but it is possible. Some one to one outdoor work involves supporting the client in solitary work. In this case it may involve the therapist meeting with the client in regular reporting sessions whilst the client undertakes a personal retreat or a series of guided exercises.

Other work may be done together, as therapist and client share time out of doors, walking or working together in a

natural environment. In the latter situation, attention to boundaries needs to be especially careful, since the possibilities for
inappropriate intimacy to be experienced or inferred are much
greater than in a consulting room. Walking with a friend or lover
in the countryside is a common activity and the therapist must
take care that such a social ambiance does not slip into the therapeutic relationship.

Co-facilitating

In this chapter, many of the comments have been predicated on
an assumption that environmentally based work will involve
two facilitators. This is prudent in that, besides the creative
input which two therapists can have, it allows for emergency
situations in which one facilitator becomes caught up in caring
for the physical or psychological needs of one of the group
members. In such circumstances the other facilitator can hold
the group process whilst their colleague responds in whatever
way is necessary.

In addition, the second facilitator can act as a sounding board
for ideas, so that exercises can be created in situ through
dialogue. This can be done in such a way that whilst the group
is engaged in one activity, the facilitators are reflecting on possibilities for the next exercise. This allows the facilitators to work
more closely with the group process, rather than pre-deter-
mining the group's direction. Such a strategy obviously depends
upon the amount of input which a particular activity requires.
Debriefing after a session gives space to reflect on the overall
process and relate the activity to theoretical perspectives.

On the other hand, it is quite possible to do work of this kind
alone provided that the group is experienced and members are
able to act responsibility in emergency situations. This latter
circumstance does have some benefits in that the facilitator who
is working on their own has a much closer relationship with the
group. For the mature group this can encourage more sharing of

responsibility and less dependency.

With co-working there may be occasions when the activity requires work in pairs. If there is an odd number of participants in the group, it can be tempting for the second facilitator to join in the activity. This can sometimes work well, but each case needs to be considered in terms of what boundaries are being affected. Different exercises involve different degrees of intimacy and personal sharing between partners.

Public spaces

Working out of doors, there is almost always a possibility, and sometimes a likelihood, of members of the public walking through the working space. This may or may not be problematic for group members. Where the group is working close to other people and unexpected meetings are likely, it is worth discussing in advance how group members wish to deal with unexpected encounters. This could include thinking through how group members might respond if they are questioned by a stranger about what they are doing.

Some groups are particularly self-conscious, and some activities will look more 'odd' to passing members of the public than others. A person who is simply sitting on a seat or walking with a companion is unlikely to raise much interest, whereas someone crawling along the ground, peering into small holes to observe insects might. It is clearly important to choose more private spots for exercises which are likely to be emotive or which involve activities that could make participants self-conscious.

Physical safety

In our own setting in France, physical safety is not generally an issue, since the site is not large and a shout would easily be heard in an emergency situation. In the event of a person not returning from an exercise, it would be relatively easy to search for them. Even here, however, we are aware of potential dangers and think through different scenarios in advance. The main risks we have identified are of someone falling and injuring themselves, of fires getting out of hand when we light them for cooking or other exercises, of snake bites (we have many adders on the land), ticks, and extremes of weather.

We discuss these at our initial briefing. There is a balance between alarming people and making them aware of possible problems. In fact many country areas have ticks and adders. We recommend suitable footwear, clothing and have plenty of 'spares' available for sudden spell of cold weather. We remind people to use sunscreen and carry water bottles if it is hot. We also ensure that there is a car available on site in the unlikely event of someone needing hospitalisation, and, as we have mobile signal on most of the site, we distribute the driver's mobile phone number in case he or she is away from the house when an accident happens.

In other settings, particularly where the work involves trips into wilder country or mountains, more precautions are necessary and the group leaders need to have suitable experience or qualifications to be able to cope with possible emergencies. Assessing risk is part of the planning process for any work of this kind.

Environmental work is healing for most people, but the type of work suggested may vary according to the needs of the group and individuals within it. For example, for people with diagnosed mental health problems there might be drawbacks to work which involves long periods of solitary contemplation, and it would be unwise to allow a group of people with such problems to spread out over too large an area. More active, inter-active work, on the other hand, is likely to be beneficial. Screening members in advance of the group by interview may therefore be advisable when a group is open to a wide cross section of the public.

This is particularly the case in groups where there will not be much verbal sharing. Talking about exercises is often not helpful as it breaks the flow of contact with the natural world and reintroduces verbalising and cognitive processing, however, working for considerable periods without verbal interaction can mean that the facilitators do not know as much about individual group members' processes as they would in a conventional therapy group. This means that the facilitators must be able to trust that the group members can be reasonably expected to cope with containing their own process during the period of the activities.

Chapter Seven

The Air Element

All our lives we breathe. Our lungs inflate, sucking in air through the nostrils and mouth, as a result of the automatic action of our muscles. The tiny air sacs, deep into the network of tubes and channels, fill with the new, fresh air, and hungry blood vessels soak up the oxygen from it into the bloodstream, exchanging it for tired old gases, the exhaust fumes of life. Then, with unrelenting inevitability, this waste carbon dioxide and the other residual gases are expelled, the lungs contracting, emptying; pushing the stale air up, out, back through the nose and mouth whence they originally came.

The process of breathing is an interesting one in that it sits on the interface between intentional and autonomic action. We can choose to change our pattern of breathing in a way that we cannot control our heartbeat or intestinal action directly, but at the same time we do not have to think in order to breathe. It is just as well, or we would spend our whole lives consciously breathing and accomplish nothing else. The body does it for us, continuing this inwards, outwards flow of air day and night and even as we sleep.

The rate of breathing varies, dictated mostly by our bodily need for oxygen. When we are active we breathe faster. When we run, we get out of breath and pant, gasping for more oxygen to feed our working muscles. When we sleep our respiration rate drops to a base level, far slower than during our wakeful hours. Occasionally our breathing gets out of sync with our needs and we hyperventilate. If we are not getting enough oxygen, when we are in a stuffy room, or when our body thinks that we should be asleep but we are not, we yawn.

Breathing varies with the emotions. Fear, anger and anxiety increase the rate of breathing as the body responds to adrenalin and other stress hormones. Stress prepares our bodies to fight or run, and for either we need more oxygen in our blood system to feed our muscles. A calm, relaxed mind-state slows the breathing as the body recovers and rests. Meditation too has this effect of slowing the breath.

The breathing is thus intimately associated with our emotional life, affected by the anxieties which we hold. The body also holds emotional associations in its posture and muscle tensions. Sometimes these tensions are described as body armouring.[20] We hold ourselves in a state of readiness, defending ourselves against the psychological or physical blows which we anticipate. Semi-permanent muscle tensions are the cumulative consequence of years of standing, moving and being in certain ways. Often they are so much a part of us that we think of them as being just how we are.

Habitual tensions associated with the breath become a part of our ongoing body-state, locking up areas of breathing so that we do not use our full lung capacity. For example, some people only move the upper part of the chest when they breathe, rarely allowing much air to enter the lower lobes of the lungs. Gases lurk there, stagnant and untapped. For such a person, deliberately breathing deeply can release great wells of emotion which have been resisted for years. This can be a difficult and painful process, but if followed through with support it may be deeply liberating. Some therapists work a lot with the breath, with cathartic results.

When we are more relaxed, however, our breathing is in a gentle harmony with our surroundings. Our body enters a quiet negotiation with our emotions, breathing sometimes driven by our psychological needs, sometimes by the body's own wisdom. Air flows between the inner and outer spaces of our bodies, replenishing and soothing muscles and mind.

Exploring the breath can help us to slow down. A key to conscious awareness, meditations often begin with the practitioner being instructed to concentrate on the breathing. We might practise counting the breaths until we reach ten, being aware of the full extent of each breath as we number it, then returning to zero, continuing to observe the flowing of air with each numbered breath. Or we might simply sit, holding the breath in our awareness.

Instructions for meditating on the breathing are found in The Setting-up of Mindfulness Sutta.[21] This sutta is so central in the Buddhist teachings that it is found twice in the early texts.[22] It starts with the Buddha teaching the monks how to use the breath as the focus of attention in meditation. He teaches them to pay attention to the quality of the breath, thinking, "Now I am breathing in a long breath, now I am breathing out a long breath; now I am breathing in a short breath, now I am breathing out a short breath," and experiencing the breath fully with each thought, and then calming it.

As we practise mindfulness of the breathing we notice the flow of air, usually following the incoming and outgoing stream of air at the space just below the nostrils. We observe the process of breathing as it naturally occurs, without judging or trying to change it. The body has its wisdom, it knows how to breathe and we can trust it to do so. We can wonder at this naturalness without interfering. "Now I am breathing in a short breath, now I am breathing in a long breath." We notice the changes and, as we do so, the breath gradually slows down.

According to the teaching, calming comes naturally from this sort of deliberate experiencing of the breath. It is not forced or imposed. As we notice the process of breathing in this slow, calm way, the body responds and becomes more relaxed under the attention. The breathing rate decreases and each breath-length increases. But it is not always the case that drawing attention to the breath brings relaxation. Sometimes the intentional observation brings anxiety. Sometimes when we practise conscious breathing we see demons which we were avoiding by tensing up our bodies. If this happens, though, we can continue to observe. Even demons change and go with attention.

The Setting-up of Mindfulness Sutta teaches the practice of breathing consciously in the context of sitting meditation. It pays attention to the way that the monk is sitting, for part of the practice is to learn to breathe well, and for this the practitioner needs an upright posture. Meditation teachers often put a lot of stress on good posture, concerned with the straightness of the spine, the angle of the pelvis and the relaxation of arms and shoulders. All of these concerns are aimed at maximising the lung capacity and stilling the body. By tilting the pelvis forwards in a half-lotus or kneeling position, the belly is extended and relaxed so that the lungs can inflate downwards. By dropping the shoulders, the upper chest relaxes and the top sections of the lungs function properly.

Mindfulness of breathing can also be practised whilst walking. As we practise walking in a grounded way, we deliber-ately cultivate consciousness of the mechanics of our feet stepping upon the earth. We can increase our awareness of our feet by consciously tuning our breath into our walking. We can imagine the breath flowing into each step. We sometimes hear this conscious walking referred to as mindful walking, but we could equally call it breathful walking. Feet and chest find their own balance of co-operation, perhaps four steps to every out breath, perhaps more. The breath soaks our energy downwards into the places where we make contact with the earth.

We breathe and share the air of this planet. On a clear day we enjoy the freshness of cool gasses filling our nasal cavities and cleansing them, inflating our lungs with life-giving energy. Other days the air is tired and polluted, unpleasant to breathe, and sometimes even causing us problems. City air can be like this, especially in less regulated parts of the world. A stuffy room, a high pollen day, smog, a main road, all remind us of the preciousness of this invisible commodity, so easily taken for granted. Contemplating the preciousness of air, we increase our tender regard for the sphere of life in which we live.

A few years ago there was a mini whirlwind in the area of our centre in France. We were in the meditation hall, walking and chanting in afternoon practice session when it struck. The day had been quiet, the end of summer, but suddenly, from nowhere, it arrived.

At first we noticed a rattling in the roof tiles and the roaring sound of wind in trees across the field. Then it hit us full on, whipping the shrubs and bushes in the yard into a frenzied tossing. Straw and chaff blew high in the air from the ground, circling outside the door of the shrine room, and there were sounds of plastic buckets and outdoor chairs bowling their way across the lawn.

We chanted on, circumambulating the room slowly as we did so. The meditation hall is open to the air. An old barn without doors, there is only the roof and walls for protection. So the wind blew in without hindrance, guttering the candles till they went out, and throwing papers and chanting books into the air. It lifted the carpets which cover the earth floor right up so that they billowed around us as we walked, their edges flapping wildly over our feet. We carried on.

The wind continued to blow, strong and chaotic, right through our session. There is something very exciting and elemental about practising in stormy weather. The sound of ancient chants competing with wind or rain or thunder is quite thrilling. It stirs our energies. I am often reminded of the line in that wonderful old hymn by John Greenleaf Whittier,[23] "Speak through the earthquake, wind and fire, oh still, small voice of calm," on such occasions.

Then, uncannily, the wind died down just as we completed

our chanting. The world returned to silence. We left the shrine room and collected the buckets and chairs. We tidied the scattered pieces of branches and leaves. The whirlwind was over.

The next day we visited our friend, Derek, who lives in the Tronçais Forest some fifteen miles away. The wind had hit there too, far worse than in our area. As soon as we arrived, he was eager to tell us how wild it had been. It had been terrifying in its ferocity as it raged around the house. In fact, it was remarkable that no roof tiles had blown off his cottage and that his tall chimney was still standing.

Then, as the weather had brightened up, Derek suggested that we go for a walk through the woods towards the lake. The main path which we usually used was closed, cut off by a strip of red and white plastic tape, but we ducked under the line and started up the track anyway. Everywhere trees were toppled at angles. Many had fallen across the path, making walking difficult. They lay higgledy-piggledy like matches scattered out of a box or a child's game of pick-a-stick. Every few yards we had to climb over a prostrate trunk or scramble through a maze of broken branches. The devastation was shocking.

It took a good half-hour to cover the short walk down to the lake shore, a walk which would normally have taken less than ten minutes. The woods were quiet now, stunned by the destructiveness they had witnessed. Soon they would be filled with the sound of chainsaws as fallen trees were salvaged by the forestry men, culled before their time.

That afternoon, the area of the forest near to Derek's house lost a third of its trees. At the time, it looked as if the whole area had been decimated, but walking in those same woods now it is hard to believe how many trees were blown over on that afternoon. The gaps have filled with new growth and the woods look as beautiful as ever. Life regenerates, and even the most devastating events are eventually healed by nature.

Climbing the hill, I pause for breath; lungs rasping, struggling to draw in enough air to feed my pounding heart. The sun is strong, relentlessly beating down on me. My chest aches with the urgency of sucking more oxygen out of the air. Doubling over, hands on knees, I pant, dragging the air, sweet and sharp, into my body as hard as I can. Then I stand recovering, replenished but tired, willing myself to be ready to head on once more, feet clambering up, up on the steep, rocky track.

Ahead I see my companion. Below, far below, the village where we set out nestles in the valley. There are several miles and a couple of hundred feet still to climb before I can once more rest on the grass of the car park. As I stop to catch my breath, I look out across the valleys.

Below me, an eagle rests upon the wind, catching a thermal and soaring up and away into the blue sky. A marmot squeals from a group of rocks higher up the slope. A cowbell jangles its deep tinny sound from somewhere down in the valley. Recovered, I continue the climb.

Air is the second of the elements. We can meditate on it as we do the other elements. There is air outside the body and air within the body.

With the breath the gases from inside and outside mingle. Air fills our lungs, but also lurks within our guts. Foul gases emerge, belched or farted into the atmosphere which all of us share. We are not cut off from our stale body elements, but circulate and re-circulate them, and those of others.

Gases exchange molecules with profligacy, the effects sometimes aesthetic, as when we smell the scent of roses or new baked bread, but other times unpleasant, or even affecting our well-being. As a community worker in the past, I used to sit in smoke-filled meetings, absorbing the out-breath of colleagues and service users, and the blue haze of their cigarette smoke, until my head swam and I felt nauseous and flushed with second-hand nicotine.

Mostly though, we are unaware of the continual exchange of gases which binds us into the web of life. One to another, we pass on the precious gift of air, sometimes freshly breathed, other times tinged with garlic, mint or putrefying intestinal flora.

Better breath-mates are plants. The photosynthetic processes are complementary to ours. We want their waste oxygen; they want our waste carbon dioxide. It works perfectly; the foundation of our eco-system. Don't mess with the plants.

Whilst I was away for a few days last week, the tear in my flysheet got worse. There was already a small rip above the doorway on the outer skin of the tent when I left. Now it is probably torn beyond repair.

When one leaves tents up all summer in the fierce sun of central France, they don't seem to last long. The nylon fabric becomes brittle after a few years and starts to be vulnerable to the slightest abrasion, splitting apart along the warp of the fibres. My tent is now in its sixth summer, so is about reaching the end of its life. It always feels wrong to jettison such a well-loved piece of equipment so soon, but in practice there is not much alternative, as, once the process of decay has started, new tears appear as fast as old ones are mended and each repair weakens the fabric somewhere else.

I did attempt to patch the split before I left with some fabric glued onto the inside of the outer tent to bridge the gap. I have done this with several other small tears in past years, but this time the glue didn't seem to hold and with the first rain my patch was on the floor and the tear was twice the size it had been previously. Indeed, I thought the split had run about as far as it could, since it had reached the seams on both sides of the flap. So it was that I left it when I went away, thinking that I would probably have a last try at stitching it when I took the tent down at the end of the summer. The hole was over the tent's porch so I didn't imagine it would come to much harm, and I had slept comfortably in it for a couple of weeks with no problems, save the need to put a plastic bowl under the gap on a couple of nights when it rained.

When I returned to France after my trip away, however, I discovered that the tent was in rather a sorry state. There had been a very high wind one night, I was told, and evidently it had got in under the flapping edges of the split, extending it sideways in several directions, so that a large hole had appeared. Shreds of tent fabric hung like prayer flags into the gaping hole. One side of the porch was effectively open to the elements, its edges peeled back by the storm. Repair seemed a much less likely prospect now. It was clear that the whole tent had become so brittle that any attempt to stitch it would only create further holes. In any case it was late evening. I had arrived home and, after the long drive from the Netherlands, I was keen to sleep. Since the inner tent was intact, I saw no reason not to sleep in my own tent.

There was something rather exciting about lying in my sleeping bag looking up, not at the grey dome of the outer tent beyond the flyscreen, but at a night sky, encrusted with sharp points of stars. Not quite sleeping in the open air, but quite close to it. A late moon was rising and soon cast its pale bright light in through the gap and onto the inner tent, creating an almost star-shaped pattern on its thin fabric, which echoed the outline of the hole with a pool of light. Pulling the sleeping bag over my head I drifted off into welcome sleep.

This morning I wake early. It has been my second night in the tent with the hole. Although yesterday I improvised a cover for the gap with some plastic sheeting, I immediately notice, from the sharpness of the early morning air as I lie in my sleeping bag, that the tent is no longer air tight. Modern tents are designed to hold the occupant's body heat and, with their double skins, create a cosy cocoon around the camper. The punctured outer shell of the tent has robbed it of this property, and the cold night air of late summer is finding its way into my sleeping compartment. My bedding is coated in a fine mist of dew and my hair feels damp too, but my body warmth has made the sleeping bag snug.

I laze, swaddled in the downy softness for a while, enjoying the clarity of the air. It is still early, maybe just after six, and I can hear a pair of owls conversing loudly not far away. Their distinctive hoots intertwine as they gossip. Eventually they fly off and I am left with just the distant sound of occasional cars on the main road a couple of kilometres away. The light is beginning to change, though the moon is still bright, hanging over the front of the tent now. I think of the coming autumn and the changes which will happen as the seasons circle on. Already there is a melancholy mistiness in the mornings and swifts and swallows are starting to congregate. It is easy to get maudlin. I decide to get up.

Stepping out into the still morning air, I see that the sun has not yet risen. There is an orange gold glow on the eastern horizon against the clear, indigo sky overhead. The quarter moon is high in the sky above the yard, white and luminous. It is not fully light.

There is something indefinably delicate about the early morning air. Its fresh chilled quality cuts through one's sleepiness. There is a penetrating silence and a sharpening of perception which is difficult to describe without falling into cliché. It affects all the senses. It is as if it coats every sound and scent and sensation with a thousand glistening dewdrops, like diamante, hard, sharp and beautiful, mirroring the experience a hundredfold. It electrifies the nerves, stunning the body into wakefulness even if the mind is sluggishly wanting to return to sleep. It fills the passages of the airways with life-giving breath, so cool and clear that it seems to scour out every stale molecule of slumber.

I walk back to the house, my feet picking up bits of wet cut grass from the orchard as I go. It is quiet. I am first to rise. I tiptoe inside. The air in the corridor is still warm from yesterday's sun. It soothes me with its comfortable familiarity after the shock of the cold dawn air. No one is yet stirring. I enjoy the peace of early morning.

Mauna Kea is 14,200 feet high. A volcano on Big Island, Hawaii, it hosts some of the world's biggest astronomical observatories. It is also a sacred Hawaiian site.

Climbing to the summit of Mauna Kea, the road winds its way up the mountain, cutting through scrubby trees and dusty volcanic desert. There is a stopping point halfway at which a large red and white sign warning of altitude sickness strongly advises the visitor to stop and acclimatise. The air at the top of the mountain is thin, and driving up does not give us time to adjust. Like so many modern inventions, the car speeds the body past its natural pace of adjustment and levels of tolerance. We stop for half an hour and wait. Wait for our breath-souls to catch up. Then we drive on.

At the top of the mountain, we are in a different world. We have climbed above the clouds and, looking down, their billowing masses hang on the primeval jungle of trees that cling to life on the lava fields. The landscape is now completely arid. Red, ochre and grey cones of volcanic ash rise above deserts of dusty ground of the same earthy colours. The sky is deep, vibrant blue. Against it, the reds and oranges are bright and sharp.

At the top of the mountain are the observatories. They are white hemispherical buildings, scattered between the huts and boxy living quarters used by the scientists, which are also white. We get out of the car, equipping ourselves with hats and sunscreen against the high ultraviolet sunlight which you get at this altitude.

Immediately as one starts to walk at over four thousand metres one becomes aware of the thin air. The extra-terrestrial quality of the sparse, colourful landscape is magnified by the dreamlike state induced by low oxygen levels in the brain. We are to walk half a mile to the sacred lake where native Hawaiians used to bring the umbilical cords of their babies. These tiny lengths of fleshy tubing, through which flowed the essence of life, were thrown into the waters there.

Although no great distance at sea level, half a mile in high altitude conditions becomes a challenging trek. We set out, keeping a slow steady pace. Each step feels as if it is made through treacle. The foot is lifted, moved through the air, and placed with a deliberateness which tells of the effort involved. Some of the effort, though, is not even felt. The dreamy mind-state becomes euphoric, noticing with curiosity that the heart is pounding at double rate and breathing is faster than usual.

We plod slowly up a huge orange-brown dust slope, like Arabs in the desert, enveloped in headscarves and long-sleeved overshirts against the sun. One by one we reach the ridge and see over it into the hollow which contains the highest lake in the United States. The view is spectacular. Red cliffs streaked with blacks and dark browns tower behind it on one side, and a boulder-strewn edge rises on the far side. Virtually nothing grows. Finding the occasional straggling plant is like finding life on Mars. In fact, the landscape could be Mars, it is so surreal and different.

We cannot stay long in the thin air. Ten minutes walking round the sacred lake, and we are ready to walk back to the car and to start our long descent to normal oxygen-rich air. Our foray into the upper levels of the earth's atmosphere has stretched our bodies to near the limits of ordinary functioning and made us acutely aware of how narrow a band of atmos-phere we are adapted to. A few thousand metres of height takes humans to the edge of liveable conditions.

Strangely though, as I descend, I miss the clarity of the high mountain air. Below the cloud line, the air is warm and humid, for we are on the east side of the island which receives exceptionally high rainfall. It is also loaded with pollens to which I have allergies. At sea level I am struggling to breathe for other reasons. My time on the mountain has given me respite from these trials. I miss the strange ethereal beauty of walking in thin air.

Chapter Eight

Encounter and Investigation

There are snails along the path as we walk across the field this morning. Yesterday's rain has turned the cut hay that lies in clumps where the mower folded it aside into a soggy mulch. The snails congregate to feed on it.

La Ville au Roi, the hamlet of two houses of which our centre is one, is famed locally for its escargots.

"Ville au Roi escargots... mmmm," the French local says, with an almost caricatured smack of the lips and doffing of pursed fingers, when he discovers in conversation at the local bar that we are the English who bought the old fermette a couple of kilometres north of the village.

It is something of a tragedy for locals therefore that Buddhists bought the house and land and declared an amnesty for the snails. "It's a conservation area for snails," I explain to monsieur the chimney sweep when he sidles up with his plastic bucket after the yearly ritual cleaning of our chimneys, asking if he could just *ramasse* a few escargots. He frowns, uncomprehending, and slopes off sulkily.

So this morning the snails are out in force. Some are solitary, but mostly they seem to hang out together in pairs, sometimes in uninhibited passionate abandonment, other times in small groups, clustered around some particularly juicy, and sometimes unsavoury, find. Excrement, dropped by a fox or other night creature which also evidently walked this path, seems particularly popular.

These snails are the large sort: big pale brown shells that spiral outwards from their tiny beginnings, the colour of the limestone rock on which they live. Once whilst I was digging in the garden I found a fossilised snail, broken out of the stone, a reminder that snails have lived here far longer than we have. The shells are ridged with rings, darker brown stripes added with each successive period of growth. Some shells are dark, some lighter, verging on pink, for the snails are individual, each patterned with its own particular markings.

The snails move on pale grey-brown bodies that extend out from their shells, delicate, with soft, fluid underbellies on which they glide, sensuously reaching out to encompass the next half centimetre of ground, then sliding forwards surreptitiously. Scored with a network of furrows, their bodies look almost scaled, yet at the same time fleshy, sleek and infinitely reactive. Though slow and methodical in traversing the ground, a snail can retract its antennae or change direction, pulling back into the safety of its shell in moments. It can also cover a distance at surprising speed if it wishes. Mostly, though, these snails do not move far, but munch on, savouring their early meal.

There is something impressive about a large snail in full sail along the path. The image of sailing fits, for the gliding movement on the one undulating foot is smooth as a schooner on a gently rolling sea. I step carefully around the wanderer, but then, on afterthought, turn and pick it up by the shell. In shock it pulls back into its hideaway, scrunching its body back inside the vaulted haven that it provides. I gently throw the creature into the soft, long grass of the field where it will be safe. It is all too easy for someone in the line walking behind me, caught up with a sound or sight somewhere out across the landscape, to accidentally step on the snails, breaking their shells with an irreversible crunch. I have done it myself. The feeling of a breaking shell beneath the feet and a life extinguishing into a mass of slimy flesh is shocking, cutting through one with the reaffirmation of our destructive nature.

After starting to write about snails, I am interrupted by a request to join in a walk across the site with some other members of the community. As so often, I become aware, in going out from my computer to walk in the natural world, that, as a result of the writing, I am seeing more detail in my surroundings. The writing has sharpened my attention for snails, and I see them everywhere: nut-brown shells half buried in vegetation, variegated shells against a mossy log, baby snails, tiny, with elongated shells.

There are striped brown and white snails of a different variety. A number of flat stones lie, half buried in the ground where we are walking, and around them I see fragments of these brittle brown and white shells, scattered about on the grass, evidence that thrushes are using the rocks as anvils to break open these snails and eat their bodies. The thrushes do not seem to tackle the big, edible snails for which our land is known though. Their shells are tougher and harder to break.

In the wood I find one snail with a scar circling half its shell, a deformity that has created a deep ridge running round the outer third of its circumference. Do snail-shells heal from damage, or did this particular snail grow that way? I become curious. Then beside the old canal ditch, along a muddy, ivy edged path, I meet a snail on the move. Antennae stretched forward to full length, it cruises on its trail of slime. I stand transfixed by its elegance. It stretches out its long, smooth, Bryl-Creemed neck, patterned with its characteristic grey mottling, whilst delicately extending its frilled margins, sliding over the dead oak leaves of the forest floor on its own lubrication. From my great height I look down at this creature with whom I share this planet, knowing that communication between us is just as impossible as if it had arrived from outer space. How does one encounter a snail?

And yet, here in the woods, we do encounter. We meet with and take interest in many small creatures. Some see us and are wary. Humans are after all the largest predator they are likely to meet. Most go on their way, oblivious to our presence. We are to them as trees or plants or rocks, large features to be climbed or walked around or avoided.

We meet them on our terms usually, and perhaps, sometimes, we can also honour these beings by appreciating that this is so. Perhaps sometimes we can at least acknowledge the difficulty of meeting them on their own terms. We are in their space, just as much as they are in ours. In theory as an intelligent species we are better placed to bridge the gap than they. Perhaps by pausing from time to time we at least reach some insight into our limitations.

Observing the detail of the natural world can be a surprising and often moving experience. We find great beauty as well as curious occurrences when we change our perspective. A friend, Richard, writes:

> In recent times I've taken to carrying a hand lens, usually of magnification X10, around with me. The incredible micro world at the heart of flowers, or the iridescence of fallen magpie feathers for example. Or insects such as ants (these are a bit tricky as they refuse to pose!), rain beetles' wing casings, are stunning to look at up close.

We rush through life, missing the detail. Environmental work invites us to slow down, take time, and look more closely. It can be about getting down on our hands and knees and peering into the hidden spots, finding the small treasures which lie among the grass or on the stream bed.

Today we are in the dance circle. We have walked down through the winding tracks among the young oaks and reached the cut area beneath the mature oak trees. Here we assemble in the big sloping field for the day's activity. Today we are exploring what it means to encounter others in this detailed way.

Sundari and I invite the group to divide into pairs and give instructions. In each pair, one person will choose to study ants, the other will study spiders. They will have twenty minutes reconnaissance time before moving on to the next part of the exercise. During that time, they will spread out through the field, observing their respective subjects.

In the field are many spiders and many ants of different sorts. One could spend hours watching them, for there are lots of different varieties of each. Some of the ants build huge mounds out of soil and grass, honeycombs of earth tunnels, highly organised with places where larvae and food are stored in specially constructed chambers. These seem to be the dwellings of larger ants. Other ants inhabit underground tunnels, crevices beneath rocks, or live under bark or in hollow places in decaying trees. Their colonies operate collectively, with ants communicating quite complicated messages to one another. There are big ants and small ants, ants of different colours. To study ants seriously is a lifetime's task.

Because of the complexity of their communal systems, anthills seem to be wonderful organisations. It is tempting to compare them with our cities. There are indeed parallels, but there is also a danger of taking the comparison too far and anthropomorphising the species, appropriating our observations to confirm our human agendas. There are always dangers in studying other creatures that we over-identify with them. Because we are programmed to seek out self-confirmation both on an individual and collective basis, we are always on the lookout for, and pleased to find, situations and objects which hold up a mirror to our selves.

Conversely, at other times we objectify the subjects of our observation, making living creatures into functional things and forgetting their sentient nature. They become objects of our desire or sources of irritation to be eliminated.

The exercise of encountering involves trying to put this identification or objectification aside and observing the creature in as neutral a way as possible. More than this, it involves letting the life before us speak to us in its own terms. Humans are very ready to anthropomorphise the things we see. From childhood we are presented with tales of talking animals; wily creatures which act in similar ways to ourselves, but better. We make sense of animal behaviour in terms of its parallels with our own, ascribing sentiments which may or may not be accurate. We talk to dogs and cats and imagine they understand English, even if they happen to live in France.

Here we try to look more cleanly, to see without interpretation, and to get beyond our suppositions. We ask, what is really happening? What is true?

In the field one can observe the anthills, but when they are intact, these show very little of their interior complexity. They simply look like piles of earth. Sometimes, however, the mower has cut through one accidentally and the colony has been broken open. Then the ants' activity suddenly becomes visible. When the hill is first broken, scores of ants appear, apparently from nowhere, rescuing their precious larvae, white cocoons as big as they are, and repairing the ruptured walls. In our field there are a few such broken mounds along the paths which have recently been cut. Since the mowing was done a few days ago, some of the broken hills seem abandoned, but others still contain ants which can be seen running about among the broken chambers.

More ants are scurrying about on the ground underneath the oak trees on the lower margin of the field where we have created our working area. At first sight these ants seem to be disorganised. Watching them, however, one soon realises that many are in fact following criss-crossing paths through the grass. They scuttle to and fro, retracing the same routes again and again. Sometimes they follow other ants, responding their scent-based signals. Help is needed somewhere else, and the ants tell one another by rubbing their antennae together.

The ants' routes converge in places into what can only be

described as ant motorways; solid lines of ants, passing each other, walking single file. Often these seem to lead to the ants' nests, which are hidden in the ground in the adjacent woodland, other times they climb up into the trees, maybe to find food in the new shoots at the tips of the branches, or perhaps they are going to an aerial nest. Lines of ants snake across areas of leaf debris. Sometimes there is a change of direction and the whole line reorganises itself. One ant discovers a new food source and soon everyone is heading towards it, diverting the stream of bodies to the new route.

Ants always seem busy. Sometimes they carry objects which are bigger than they are. Heavy, awkward items weave through the maze of grass stems, swaying from side to side as the ant bearer struggles with the effort. I have seen ants moving butterfly wings from place to place, like giant yacht sails towering over them, or pieces of grass many times their own size, held aloft like giant cabers.

The ants which we are observing often seem to be carrying the corpses of other ants. Perhaps it is because we have been working in the area and have trodden on many of them that they spend so much time undertaking. When we start to look closely at the natural world and realise how thoughtless and destructive we are it is easy to feel guilty.

Sometimes the ants work on their own, other times they work co-operatively. Once, when I was picnicking in a roadside lay-by, I noticed a group of ants working to manoeuvre an almond flake, presumably discarded by a previous picnicker, into a hole in the ground. In the end it took them three hours to achieve this. I watched them, fascinated. At first it seemed they had taken on an impossible task, for the almond was many times bigger than they were, but they persisted. They moved the almond back and forth, turning it and trying it this way and that, nibbling the edges off to make it fit into the hole. Eventually they managed it, dragging it out of sight into the ground. I felt like cheering as I saw it go.

Ants never seem to stop their activity. Spiders on the other hand seem to spend a lot of time sitting, waiting for their prey to arrive. Whilst ants forage for their food, once their webs are built, spiders allow their food to come to them. They can move quickly, but much of the time they don't move at all.

There are many large spiders in the field, yellow bodied, with black stripes circling their abdomens. Walking across the open grassy areas they are easy to spot. Their dramatic patterning stands out against the green of the plants. They are the kings of the field, the ones who deck the grasses with shimmering plates of dew drops in the mornings, their giant webs spanning the spaces between the stems with great wheels of concentric gossamer. It is one of the great pleasures of the French centre to walk out around the meditation path on a September morning when the chill of night is still in the air and the spiders have been at work. The field glistens with their jewelled nets. At such times it becomes apparent just how many of them there are.

The yellow spiders spin large round webs, classic spider's web shapes, with a thicker zigzag of thread near the centre. They work at night, for their webs are always pristine in the morning.

Other sorts of spiders are smaller, brown and reticent. They build misty veils of nests deep among the bases of the grass stems. Some of these have quite complex constructions, with gauzy tunnels in which their owners hide, waiting for their prey to arrive. It is easy to miss these tiny traps, but once again, the morning dew reveals them, misted with water droplets.

In the woods yet other sorts of spiders spin the yarns that loop across the paths between the trees, long strands which catch one's face as one walks, draping it with sticky cobwebs. These spiders sit to one side of their webs, crouching against the tree to which the web is attached, ready to pounce upon the unfortunate insect which lands on their web and envelop it in sticky threads to create their food store. You can often see the hanging parcels of corpses, carefully wrapped and suspended beside the web.

The sound of the bell brings the researchers back. They return to their pairs where they discuss their findings. For this exercise we use a method called role reversal, a technique borrowed from psychodrama.24. In this the participants each take on the roles of the creatures which they have been researching and try to explain how the world looks through that creature's eyes. They play the parts of ants or spiders. It is a light-hearted activity, yet serious too, if only in the fact that it demonstrates just how difficult it is to explore the perspective of another species. Can you be a spider? Can you be an ant? Can one even start to get into the mindset of such a different creature? Does an ant or a spider have a mindset at all? The group begin to realise how human-centred their perspective is. The exercise gives them an opportunity to share their discoveries but it also highlights how much of the lives of other beings they cannot penetrate.

The pairs engage in animated dialogue, having fun as the two creatures banter. It is impossible to really get into the respective minds of ants and spiders, as their attempts to do so demonstrate, but the exercise encourages the group members to draw on their observations and justify the viewpoint of the creature they have been studying with evidence gleaned from the researches.

A couple of days later we are working in a different field. This time we are in the fire circle, which is in a grassy field on top of the hill, surrounded by woods of oak and field-maple. I ask the group to return to their roles as ants or spiders, and explore how the respective creatures behave in this different terrain. They disperse once more to carry on their research.

Here the ants build even bigger mounds and the spiders spin huge webs between the larger saplings in the open field.

We also find a wasps' nest being built down among the long grass stems. It is in the earliest stages. About the size of a man's fist, its structure of layered combs is still visible, as the paper coating has not yet been created. We watch as the wasps come and go. Life swarms around us; so many species of insect, and most unidentified at least by us. Beetles and bugs, damselflies and moths flutter and jump around us. The air is full of grasshopper sounds. Every inch of grass seems to be alive.

It is easy enough to talk romantically about encountering nature, but when we look more closely at the creatures around us, the idea of really encountering them becomes complicated. The lives of animals and birds and insects can be observed, studied and recorded but too often the subjects of our study simply become our resources. They are objectified. Their living presence becomes meaningless as they become commodities, subjected to human-centred theorising or used to reflect our self-interested views. Real encounter respects the mystery of others, acknowledging the unbridgeable gap between us, whilst yet attempting to achieve some sort of understanding of that other's reality.

Chapter Nine

Myth and Imagination

This morning we stay within the yard for our first session. The yard is a large area, faced on one side by the old farmhouse, a one-story building, with three rooms downstairs and a large granary above, and the barn where we store our outdoor tools and building materials. On the opposite side there is an older barn. It is built of the same honey coloured limestone and rendering, and has a large rectangular entrance at the front, which sticks out from the main body of the building, open to the elements, with a pitch roof set on a triangular timber frame that is visible from outside.

This older barn is now our meditation hall, but it was a ruin when we first came here seventeen years ago. The roof had fallen in at one end, leaving exposed skeletal timbers which stood up against the sky like a stage set from a Hollywood horror film. Inside it an elder tree was growing in the midst of the debris of fallen tiles and the crumbling remains of animal stalls and rotting hay. We cleared it out, barrowing the rich residues left by its previous occupants onto our compost heaps to enrich the poor soil of the garden. Then we spent a summer demolishing the last sections of the old roof. This was a rather alarming job which involved setting up scaffolding and clambering along the tops of the old walls to dislodge the remaining timbers from where they were cemented into the stone. They would fall with almighty crashes into the shell of the building, creating resounding shockwaves through the floor and walls and sending up clouds of dust. Once this demolition was done, we got a local builder to replace the roof with a new one.

The yard has lots of interesting corners and features in it. There is a pond to one side of the meditation hall. This was dug out by a couple of volunteers many summers ago, and it is deep enough for a man to stand shoulder height in. It has to be this way so that fish can survive the severe winters that we get here. There is always air trapped under the ice, even if it freezes over.

We once had six fish in it, but now only one remains, a large red and white koi carp, whose golden lips sometimes majestically break the surface of the water to suck at the water lily leaves or pull the grass that fringes the edge. The others, we think, were victims of a snake which took up residence in the pond a few years back. It used to circle on the surface of the water with a proprietorial air, swimming elegantly, head held high, gliding in serpentine curves, or sometimes diving down to swim completely under water if it sensed that we were watching. It too has now disappeared, leaving just the fish, some water boatmen and a very fine green frog.

This frog is a recent arrival who appeared in the spring. A solitary wanderer, it is not clear how he got here, but, once established, he made his presence audible. His melodious croaking kept conversation with the neighbour's dogs for all the early part of the summer, until eventually he gave up hope of a mate and fell silent. He is still around though. We often hear the plop as he leaps into the water when we pass.

Beside the pond, in a small walled bed, are lavender plants, now rather straggly and old like miniature wizened trees, but still giving us a good crop of flowers each year. We cut them early whilst the scent is at its best, and hang them in bunches in the guest rooms or dry them in the sun to make lavender bags. The smell lasts for years, and is a powerful relaxant.

The flower beds in the yard are rather wild. They are left to fend for themselves during the winter months, and only the hardiest, most unruly plants survive in them. For the most part this means herbs. Marjoram sows itself and grows into big clumps with purple flowers and masses of green foliage. Sage and rue, planted when we first arrived, have both grown into well-established bushes over the years, though our rosemary plant only just hangs on, having grown lean and thin. Lemon balm colonises big areas of the beds, competing with stinging nettles that tend to invade the whole area. Further down the yard, in front of the barn, a patch of ginger mint has naturalised itself between the grasses. Its more delicate leaves are wonderful in salads and with rice noodles, Vietnamese style.

Underfoot, the ground is surprisingly varied. Some is grassy, cut short in the lawn area, but left long and unkempt in some of the rougher places at the edges of the yard. Other parts are covered with broken tile from the demolished roof or with loose gravel. There are patches of bare stone in the centre of the yard where vehicles come and go, where the bedrock is exposed, the top soil having been worn away with years of traffic; carts and horses before motorised vehicles. There is also an area of crazy paving in front of the house, laid down by volunteers some years ago and now weathered in.

The yard is edged in several places by drystone walls, low and a little ramshackle, having been for the most part inexpertly created by members of the community. Plants make up other boundaries. There is a broad-leafed bamboo beside the pond. Three cherry trees, an apple and a flowering plum grow at the end furthest from the meditation hall in a patch of grass which serves as a lawn. A forest of fennel plants, taller than a person, grows alongside another walled area, where a spiral sculpture was made out of roof tiles several years ago. This spiral is still there, invaded by weeds and suckers from the cherry trees.

With its variety of small habitats, this area is ideal for the exercise which Sundari and I have in mind today. We are looking for a space where the group can spread out and yet remain within earshot of one another, and where they can find miniature spaces for imaginative work. The yard therefore seems particularly well suited to this sort of small-scale working.

Today we are working with myth, but we are also interested in inviting group members into an experience which challenges their sense of sizes and scales too. Changing the scale provides a different way of unsettling assumptions. Because we are used to relating to things within our own size frame, being invited to restrict our interest to a very small area reminds us to look more carefully at the details of our environment, as well as demonstrating how human-centred our view of scale is. It can be a sobering experience. If we overlook so much in a tiny space, how much more do we fail to notice as we go about the world, which itself consists of many such spaces, in our usual way.

Initially the group are invited to spread themselves about the yard. Each person is asked to find a small piece of the space that interests them. It should be no more than a foot or two across, a forgotten corner or marginal space in which imagination can be allowed to play. Because the area is so diverse there are plenty of spaces to choose from. Once they have found their spot, we tell people that they are to sit or lie in front of it, contemplating it.

By instructing people to sit or lie, we make sure that it will be apparent to us as facilitators when everyone has chosen their location. Getting down to ground level is also functional to the exercise as it immediately provides a new perspective from which the chosen spot is viewed.

Once everyone is in place, the group members are told to imagine that the small area which they have chosen is in fact a piece of land which is inhabited by creatures about the size of ants. This invitation thus transforms the spot into a world in miniature, a landscape in which unknown inhabitants live and move about. They are asked to imagine that they are viewing this world as if from a great distance or from a height, maybe from the perspective of a giant being or maybe from some flying vantage point. Entering into this strange new world, they are to imaginatively create a mythical land, drawing on their observations, but allowing their imagination to play freely. Perhaps this world is in another time and space. The creatures which live there have very different lives from those of humans. Or perhaps there are similarities between the mythic world and our world, uncanny parallels made strange by its different territory.

Before the group disperses to start the exercise, I demonstrate what I have in mind. For this, I identify a crack between some paving stone slabs near to where we are standing. It is filled with dusty red earth and a few sparse plants. I let my imagination loose. These plants might be trees, growing in a desert landscape, within a huge canyon. I point out the features, and as I do so, feel myself growing immensely tall. It suddenly feels as if I am in an aeroplane looking down on a miniature landscape. Perhaps the area at the bottom of the canyon is a dried-up river and a creature living there is making a journey along its banks... I could continue but this is enough to give the group an idea of what is expected so I stop.

The group scatter about the working space. Some find places around the perimeter of the yard, holes in walls or spaces among the rough grass. Others settle on the uneven ground in the middle of the yard or move to the edges of the garden where there is bare earth. Some of the group members find their places quickly. Others take a while. Eventually everyone is settled.

Sundari and I sit, silently watching as they spend time contemplating their chosen spots.

After about ten minutes I invite the participants to choose partners. They do this by making eye contact in the silence. I tell them to come and stand close to me, together with their partners. In this way everyone leaves their mythic world and comes back to the centre of the yard before moving on to the next stage of the activity.

Now the participants are to take it in turns to lead their partners back to their spaces and introduce them to the worlds which they have imaginatively created. They go and sit down together in front of one of the partners' spots and the host tells their visiting partner the story of their mythic place and its inhabitants. When this is finished, they visit the other partner's place.

An exercise like this is fun, creating an interlude between more intensive group activities, but it has a serious purpose too. It frees the imagination and challenges habitual ways of viewing things. It also brings into focus ordinary things which are easily overlooked. It feeds creativity, stretching people's imagination. People tend to look at the world in ways that can be quite dismissive. We notice something and mentally label it, and then move our attention on to the next object which presents itself before we have really looked at the first one. Often we hardly see things at all because we assume we know what they are and so do not look properly.

Buddhist psychology speaks of this in terms of the functioning of the conditioned senses. Our senses are not under our control, but, like a crowd of rowdy youngsters, dart about, grasping at objects that support their preferred way of seeing or hearing. This preferred way is ultimately concerned with creating a sense of self. So the whole world becomes *lakshana*[25] for us; it is viewed not for its own sake, but in ways that indicate identity. These processes, according to Buddhist psychology, are not conscious. They are not linked to thought processes, but are conditioned into the senses themselves.

The exercise is imaginative. It uses observation of reality as a jumping-off point from which to elaborate creative ideas and build fantasies. In doing this it invites reflection on the habitually human-centric viewpoints which we adopt most of the time. Playing with scale contributes to this process, for the scale and angle from which we generally view things is not determined by some objective reality, but, rather, is conditioned by our particular size and structure as human beings. Taking on the scale of an ant, our perception of the terrain changes and different features within it become significant.

Things which are part of the human world-view become so large that they disappear into abstraction, just as the continents and oceans of this planet are invisible to people because their scale is beyond our viewpoint. Without the vantage points of maps and space, in our direct experience all that appears is land and sea. Continents and oceans are merely concepts. The way that these larger geological features are created out of land and sea is invisible because of its scale and can only be appreciated through cognitive effort and theoretical understanding. So too, in this miniature world, a new landscape emerges out of dust and pebbles whilst the continents of fields and mountains ranges of buildings disappear from view.

Changing our viewpoint and letting go our habitual assumptions about the world shakes our certainty, opening our minds to new possibilities. We enter a new space in which we don't know the rules. We have to look more closely and try to make sense of what we see, interpreting it on the basis of building blocks of prior experience, but observing more carefully and living on our wits. In the process of creating a mythical world, although in one sense we know that we are playing with ideas and stories, in another we loosen our attachment to knowing what things are. Paradoxically, in creating the fiction, we look more carefully at what is in front of us in order to spot the tiny details on which to hang the story. Giving up assumptions encourages us to look with fresh eyes. We search for the odd, the beautiful and the interesting.

Stories grow in the telling. In the sharing circle after this exercise, several group members note that they had only a sketchy idea of their mythic world and the stories associated with it when they first got together with their partners. It was the other person's presence which acted as a catalyst to creativity. When instructed to tell their partner about the world they had created, they felt pressure to come up with a good story, so embellished the tale which they had previously thought of, entering more fully into the scene they were describing as they recounted the story of their imaginary world to their companion. Showing the miniature world to their partners, they took on the tour guide's attention for the detail of landscape, features and history.

Storytelling is a co-creative process, a shared activity of the storyteller and the listener. It is always so. Even in writing fiction, the author is conscious of the invisible reader, who questions, encourages and challenges her to convey the tale more excitingly, more clearly, more vividly, avoiding boring detail and bringing the scenario to life.

But myths are also reflections of a deeper truth. They draw deeply on those layers of mental process which are hidden beneath our everyday thought. Some myth speaks to personal preoccupations. Habitual thinking, scripts, unconscious dreams and longings all emerge in myth. The plasticity of story makes it a mirror in which the preoccupations of people's lives can be reflected. Without knowing it, the storyteller reveals him or herself. All fiction is autobiographical.

Also, though, myth is not so much an individual medium, but rather it is a product of the collective process. Although we may draw on personal versions of these truths, in myth we discover the commonality of human experience. The deepest archetypal layers of myth are universal. It is for this reason that they hold universal appeal. Myth deals with the stuff of life, the common scripts of birth and death and struggle; of loves and losses, journeying and homecomings, conflicts and peacemaking. So it is that in these miniature kingdoms we discover common roots of human experience played out in personally rooted variations.

And, of course, in an exercise such as this one, miniature worlds take many of us back to childhood experiences. We are reminded of the games we played, creating secret places and fantastic worlds in which we could act out different possibilities. In this light-hearted creative exploration we revisit our childhood selves, retrieving our capacity to play and dream. Maybe we find other long-forgotten treasures too. As adults, the exercise allows us to experience once again the magical times we had as children when things could be other than ordinary and dragons walked the earth.

These exercises cultivate our capacities to look, to communicate, to dream. They start a journey which can lead us back out into the wilder spaces, or into creative work of other forms: art, drama, writing and so on. In itself, though, such an exercise is contained and can be complete as what it is. It can provide starting points for further work to build on or it can remain a simple imaginative exercise, building observation skills and challenging our adult habits of dismissing these forgotten corners of the environment.

The mythic world is commonly depicted in scenes which are closely aligned with nature. Whether Lord of the Rings or Avatar, the use of natural imagery as a backdrop lends atmosphere and associations to the narrative. Forests and mountains, rivers and great lakes, magical beasts and elemental forces all appear in traditional and modern fairy tales as players in the drama.

When we work in natural places, we therefore draw on a rich reserve of archetypal imagery, which can in turn enable the world of myth to come alive. Imaginative and traditional material can be used in new, expansive ways, drawing on folk traditions and the countercultural ideas, legacies of earlier times passed down orally in song or tales or superstitions. Moving in different types of terrain, the resonances between mythic themes and the environment can inspire creative work and imaginative introspection.

The effect which different spaces have upon us is sensed at

both cognitive and visceral levels. We feel and breathe spaces as much as we name and describe them. Entering a wood, for example, we feel the proximity of trees at a bodily level; we sense the quality of light between their branches, the presence of trailing creepers or tangled undergrowth, and the darker forms of life which live on the forest floor. We can explore such experience consciously, reflecting on phenomena which we observe, but more, we can explore it viscerally, allowing ourselves to sense the feeling tone or ambiance of a place, which is often hard to put into words. When we do this, the wood creates an emotional presence. It embraces us or threatens us, invites us or challenges us.

This is something which we most likely experience all the time at some level, but we are probably not generally conscious of these feelings, which lurk in the edges of our consciousness like phantoms. Such feelings do influence us, however. They may affect whether we return to a place, or which direction we take along a path. We feel lifted by some environments and depressed by others, fearful or agitated in some and relaxed in others. These feelings are given voice in myth. Thus myth reveals underpinnings of truth which is often beyond the reach of our conscious minds.

Allowing the imagination to play, these feeling states can be explored and this can form the basis for creative and therapeutic work. Places can provide the starting point for many kinds of creative work. The wood, for example, could become the inspiration for dramatic enactment. The feeling it evoked, its spatial qualities and features, its different vistas, all offering inspiration for play. The spirits which inhabit such a space, ghosts of the past or future, brought in by those engaging in the work or lurking, waiting to be discovered, might be personified. In an enactment of the forest, characters such as tree spirits and goblins, light faeries and terrifying giants might emerge. Such places could also inspire art or poetry, as the associations and the emotional tenor which they evoke are expressed in colour or idiom.

Different times of day bring particular associations. I recently took a walk through Tronçais Forest at dusk with a few companions. There was a moon rising, nearly full and very bright, low on the horizon. We glimpsed it through the trees as we walked, a sharp yellow light shattered by the overlapping branches. In the distance we could hear the bellowing of stags, already seeking out their autumn mates. Their calling was plaintive, haunting yet powerful with the energy of their masculinity. The path which we took through the forest was familiar. It was one we have walked many times. Yet it was still difficult to follow the track in the gathering darkness as we passed through places where the trees grew thickly. The night was closing in.

Many stories start with such a scene. Perhaps they tell of the lone traveller, anxiously seeking a place of safety, or maybe of the hunter stalking his prey in the darkness. Perhaps they tell of the time when spirits roam and souls are restless; of dangerous supernatural forces, or of protective energies. When we are close to sleep, such times drift into our minds as we hover between the realms of waking and dreams, swathing reality in a cloak of other-worldly images. Nightfall holds such qualities.

On the other hand, dawn is a time of clarity. As the air becomes most chill, the first glimmerings of light appear in the eastern sky. It is long before sunrise. Shadows and forms still play in the half-light, but the forest is waking in its chorus of birdsong. Even as the last owls are winging their way home, their haunting calls telling of a night spent hunting and animals rustle in the undergrowth, louder than their size predicts, the stars become fainter and one by one fade into the steely sky. Gradually light returns. Dew glistens in the air and on the leaves of ferns. The spiders rest from their night's endeavours. The coming of daylight is herald to many religious rites. It is a common time for births or deaths to occur, a time of transition and new beginnings. Pale and bright, insight emerges as the cold light of day breaks.

Sunset, on the other hand, paints the world with a calm and sometimes melancholic tone. Heroes ride off into the West, and old souls depart. It is a time when light transmutes to darkness, almost faerie time, when stories are told around the embers of the campfire.

The natural world gives opportunities for exploring mythic themes overtly. Creative work and ritual performances often draw consciously and intentionally on story and myth. Themes can be developed and discussed or used as illustration for the personal and the psychological.

On the other hand, sometimes this sort of work may tread more lightly amid this material, alluding only loosely to the mythic layer of consciousness but never voicing the stories or concretising the imagery. Such subtler use of the mythic dimension might be found for example in the way that language is used or in the tone of voice in which instructions are given. A facilitator may simply suggest a walk in a wood at 'faerie time' to evoke goose-bumps and a sense of unseen presences. Silence can be more powerful in inviting the mythic dimension to be present than the full telling of a tale.

The tone set by the group leader holds the space for the group's creative energies to play. If the group leader is able to 'see' the faerie folk or feel the breath of dragons, even if little is said, the tone of instructions will convey an imaginative world that is rich in imagery and dream spirits. This space is conveyed in manner more than instruction so that if for example the leader gives an invitation 'to follow along the path in silence, watching and listening, looking out lest creatures seen and unseen are prowling', this communicates to the group that this is a space where imaginative experience is valued.

Mythic work straddles the space between the personal and

the collective, drawing on themes which are part of the common heritage of our culture, and embedded in our human experience so deeply they seem to rise from the coding of our genetic make-up itself. Whether we consciously introduce mythic figures, drawing on folk traditions and pagan rites or we explore intuitive experience and personal resonances, the use of myth adds a generous and rich underpinning to our encounter with the natural world.

Chapter Ten

Attraction and Aversion

We construct our sense of who we are and of the world which we inhabit out of our selective habits of perception. In other words, as we go through life our attention is constantly drawn to things which either support our sense of identity because we perceive them as 'my sort of thing' or else define our sense of self by being something which we dis-identify from. We think, "I don't like that," or "I'm not the sort of person who would want one of those.". This identification with and rejection of the objects which we encounter happens automatically and, initially at least, on a preconscious, bodily level. It is part of being an ordinary human.

Our attention is particularly caught by objects which have importance for us. These objects have an energy which we call *rupa*. They have this power because they are associated with the process of creating our personal identity. Objects which are *rupa* are *rupa* because they are viewed in a conditioned way, and this is because in some way they fit into our story about ourselves. If you hear your name spoken across a room, your ears are caught, even though there may be many people talking, because your name has powerful *rupa* energy for you. If you feel emotional listening to a particular piece of music, it probably affects you because it is associated with part of your personal story, some past experience, such as, perhaps, an important event or relationship in your life. When you see a piece of china like the tea set which your grandmother used to use or a picture like one which your parents had on their wall when you were a child, you probably feel an upwelling of memories and associations which is powerful because the object is a part of *your* identity. All of these objects are charged with personal meaning, and so are *rupa* for you.

The quality of *rupa* is something which we perceive in the object, rather than something intrinsic to the object itself. It is a colouration which we add to an object when we identify with it. It is phenomenal rather than substantive; our personal way of viewing the world. Our response to an object which is *rupa* may be simply to increase the attention which we give to it.

Our senses are caught by the *rupa* object and fascinated by it because of its personal associations. On the other hand, our fascination with the object may be based on false assumptions. Our attention to the object may be distorted by our preconceptions about it or we may even make mistakes in viewing it. Our search for self-confirmation leads us to see what we long to see rather than what is actually there. For example, when we walk down a street of shops, we tend to notice the shop windows which have goods associated with our current interest and not see the others. The person who is interested in fashion will notice dress shops, whereas the person who has just got engaged will notice jewellers and bridal wear shops. The person who in into cars will notice the shop that sells car accessories. The person who likes books will notice bookshops, whereas the person who is on a diet will notice cake shops.

As we can see from the latter example, our attention may be caught by things which we are trying to avoid as well as things which we like. The person who is trying to lose weight wants to avoid food, but finds his or her attention constantly caught up by it. Also, the person who is dieting may see a brightly painted van at the end of the street and think that it is an ice cream van, only to discover on coming nearer that the brightly painted sign is actually advertising the owner's business and not food related at all. We joke about things like this and say, "Oh, you've just got food on the brain."

As we perceive things, so we react to them. This reaction is based on sensory experience, each sense being capable of being individually hooked by *rupa* objects. As we saw in an earlier chapter, the process whereby the self is created is formulated in the teaching of the *skandhas*. This teaching presents a five-step cycle which translates experience into a set of habitual mental activities with which we come to identify. We perceive things in a conditioned way and this informs our reaction, which in turn informs the way we behave. Our behaviour creates ways of approaching the world which then condition our view. Thus we are caught in a circular process.

The second step in the process of the *skandhas* is reaction or *vedanā*. *Vedanā* is a body response in which we respond to the object of our attention, the thing which is *rupa*. The responses are grasping, rejecting or ambivalent and/or dulled. These are the three logical possibilities for reaction: positive, negative or neutral. They are defined in the Buddhist teaching known as *the three poisons*; greed, hate and confusion. These are the three ways that we initially engagement with things.

We can note here that *vedanā* is pre-verbal. It is a reaction which occurs almost at the same moment as we perceive something. As soon as we see the dress or the new car in the shop window we are either coveting it or disliking it before we have consciously thought about it. Our eyes and body go 'wow' or 'yuck' and we feel a gulp in the stomach before we have even registered that we have seen the object to which we are reacting, if we are aware enough to notice it at all.

Working with attraction and aversion

There can be many opportunities to explore processes of attraction and aversion in a group of the kind being described here. One exercise which we have used to explore these aspects of perception in the natural environment is to send people on a *walk of awareness*, either individually or as a group. As people walk they are encouraged to notice what catches their attention.

The person walks, noting things which appear to her: tree, butterfly, grass, dead mouse, grass, flower, slug, anthill, grass, and so on. With each object there is a response. She notices this reaction. What is she drawn to, what does she reject? Some objects are noticed repeatedly, maybe because they are common things or maybe because the person has a preoccupation with the phenomenon. Not all common things are noticed however. Some things are so taken for granted that they are never named at all.

Building on this exercise, participants can work with a partner to explore the way that positive and negative attachment forms part of the process of maintaining identity. The pair walks along, with the person in front speaking out the names of objects that catch their eye and the person behind jotting them down in a notebook. At the end of the walk, the partner reads back the list and the first person indicates whether the object aroused a positive, negative or neutral response.

At this point the pair can broaden their exploration. They can discuss in what ways the first person identified with the objects she perceived. Were the things which were identified with those which had a positive response? Were the things which she dis-identified with those which were rejected? The results are not necessarily straightforward. We can see something as positive but not necessarily identify with it. We can be attracted to things which we think of as different from us. We may not recognise something as representing an aspect of our self so we may feel no conscious connection to a particular object, but another person may be able to see that it probably does have personal significance. We can identify with an object which we perceive as unpleasant because it reflects an aspect of ourselves which we don't like.

Often the reaction which we have to an object is connected to the memories and associations which we have connected with it. It can therefore be helpful to explore whether any of the objects listed have particular associations.[26]

The connection between objects and our identity may not be obvious and we may find it hard to trace associations. Often we associate or disassociate the object with something or someone who is important in our world rather than with our sense of identity. This kind of exploration is best held lightly and kept at the level of playing with possibilities rather than trying to find answers. Nevertheless sometimes this sort of exploration can offer surprising and interesting insights.

Whilst some reactions and associations are particular and personal, in the natural world our associations often touch on bigger existential preoccupations. Things we encounter catch our attention because they remind us of life and death, growth and decay. Such preoccupations are on the one hand universal, but, on the other hand, affect us personally because they threaten the foundations of our being. They evoke the anxiety and fear which arises from knowing our basic vulnerability, and the impermanence on which all life is founded.

This fear drives the creation of identity. Our attempt to control life by creating a solid sense of self is basically defensive. Fear of our own impermanence, and that of those we love, fuels our attempts to limit psychological and physical risk. It leads us to withdraw from encounter with others in various subtle and not so subtle ways. We reject things which unsettle us, both because we do not want to identify with them, and because they give rise to those feelings of existential anxiety which in the first place led us to create a sense of identity.

Nature reflects life in all its forms, and the attractions and aversions which we feel when we immerse ourselves in the natural environment may be more rooted in our generalised fears and our fantasies about these existential forces than in specifically personal memories or associations. We may be revolted by objects which are decaying or dead. For example, the experience of coming across a dead bird full of squirming maggots on the path might make us recoil. Conversely, we are attracted to flowers and new leaves which seem to suggest growth and vibrancy and carry associations of romance and festivities.

In nature the two aspects of life and death are often found together, the new growing out of the decay of the old. The rotting log brings forth fresh growth of ferns and moss. Crows find carrion in the corpses of animals by the roadside. Vegetable peelings can be composted into rich brown loam.

Images of death

In the early Buddhist community, one of the meditations commonly prescribed for the monks was to sit in meditation in the charnel grounds where dead bodies were laid out and left to decompose, contemplating the stages of decomposition of the body. This meditation was intended to remind the monks of the impermanence of the body and its eventual demise. It was said to counter lust, but it also faced the monk with sights which echoed his own mortality. Death rites are still important in modern Buddhism and the encounter with death is seen as something which may contribute to our spiritual maturity rather than being something we should avoid. Even though it may feel threatening, contact with death is something which also has the capacity to touch us and uplift us spiritually.

The recent Japanese film *Departures*, director Yojiro Takita[27] tells the story of a young man who, on returning to his home village in the rural north of Japan, looks for work to support himself and his young wife. He answers an advertisement from a company which he mistakenly thinks is a travel agency. In fact the job turns out to be working for a firm of encoffiners, a profession regarded as very lowly in Japan, which subcontracts work from undertakers. The main work involves carrying out the preparation of dead bodies for burial or cremation.

Encoffiners place the deceased person in the coffin in the presence of their relatives in a formal, respectful ceremony. This includes the ritual washing and dressing of the corpse, applying make-up and arranging the hair and clothing before sealing the coffin lid. The profession has a reputation for being distasteful, even unclean, but despite this image, the young man, and, vicariously, the audience discover that in fact the role involves performing these intimate tasks with great tenderness, preserving the dignity of the person who has died and honouring their departure from this life. In the film it becomes apparent that the young man's boss, the firm's director, is a man who came to the work through his own experience of bereavement. His work is an ongoing tribute to his former wife, as he continues to offer caring and compassion towards the families he serves.

It is a deeply moving and beautifully made film, which shows how the young man is at first appalled to discover his mistake, but gradually comes to see his work in a new way. It follows his experiences as he, at first reluctantly, accepts the job, but then gradually moves from a position of alienation and revulsion to one of sensitivity and maturity, touched by the reverence and quiet elegance of his employer's treatment of the bodies of the dead. The film is first and foremost about spiritual transformation. It shows how, through coming into the presence of death with an open heart, a person is changed.

In nature, we frequently come upon death in its different forms. A dead animal hit on the road, a rotting log covered with fungi, a sheep's skull found on the moors, a chick that has fallen from its nest and died on the ground are all reminders that life and death form one cycle. Group participants who are accustomed to city life are often unused to the immediacy of encountering such things at close quarters. They are used to driving on or walking past if they notice these things at all. In environmental therapy people can find they have the same impulses to turn away and avoid images of death but such situations may offer opportunities if the desire to flee is resisted.

One group member this summer commented that she had been revolted at the sight of a piece of rotting wood. It was slimy and unpleasant looking and made her think of death. When she looked more closely, however, she saw that on it were growing many small plants. Her feeling towards it changed. Life springs from death in the wild. New young trees grow in the crumbling remains of their parent's fallen branches.

In longer groups it can be a powerful experience to discover a dead animal and to watch its decomposition over the course of the group's life. The corpse gradually returns to its constituents and the soil, or is consumed by other creatures. The experience of observing a dead animal can be more immediate than is possible with a human death in modern times. We can look and touch. We can leave the body to decay where it was found. Animal bodies are often seen flattened on roads or tossed into the gutters in a way that would be unthinkable with human corpses.

So with dead animals we are free to observe the process of decay. The experience, though challenging, is acceptable. Although people will be emotionally affected, it will certainly be far less powerful than it would be if it were a human body the group were looking at.

This year I found a part of a snake on the path that led to my tent. At first I thought it had been cut by the mower, but I then realised that, as it was a week or more since the path had been cut and the piece of the snake's body was quite fresh, it had probably been dropped by a bird of prey. The smooth, scaled corpse lay in a grey curve across the path so that I stepped over it each time I walked back to my sleeping space. It was not patterned with the characteristic viper zigzags, so was probably part of a couleuvre, one of the larger harmless snakes which we find in our region of France. It had curving muscle bands on the underside but otherwise it was featureless.

As the days went by, gradually the snake's body was invaded by insects. The ribbing of the underside of the snake's body became more apparent. Beetles of several sorts and sizes started to hollow out the flesh so that skin was left empty, a scaly, papery shell, stiff enough to maintain its form even when there was nothing left inside. Then gradually over a week or so even these traces were eaten away. One day it was gone. There was no sign of it at all. Either the beetles had finished their job, or some other creature had taken the last remnants for a meal.

Such a process of observation can be both gruesome and fascinating. When he was about three, my son spotted a dead sheep whilst we were walking on the moors. It was a white heap of wool, slouched on its side, its back towards us. He ran towards it excitedly, for young boys are often fascinated by death, shouting out as he went, "Look, a dead sheep."

When he reached the sheep, however, he walked around it and looked at the carcass from the far side, which was turned away from us. His face changed. I wondered what he had seen. Then he came back to the family shaking his head. "It's very dead," he reported.

As we reached it, we found that most of the sheep's body had in fact rotted away and only the woolly pelt remained intact around the decomposing flesh and skeleton. It was indeed very dead.

In a group, sharing our experiences of encountering death and decay is valuable and healing. There are invariably personal memories of loss in any group. Many people have fears of dying and illness. The universality of death and sickness manifests in specifics. Sharing these personal stories and imaginings, the collective and the individual sit side by side. Through contact with the environment where the natural processes are unfolding and the experience of death is integrated with the bigger cycles of growth, change, decay and renewal, naturally facilitates the discovery of new perspectives and fosters faith.

Exploring attraction phenomena

It is difficult to know what we have not seen. By definition the unseen has been occluded by other things which we have prioritised. Because we tend to assume that our view of the world is neutral, we are unaware that our perception is in fact highly filtered.

The sort of observation exercises described earlier in this chapter can be helpful in revealing how different people interpret the world. It can be interesting, for example, to look the lists of objects which different people have noticed whilst on a walk along the same track. During the *walk of awareness* one person might be preoccupied with flowers and know the names of all of them, while another notes the light quality and the colours and a third notes sounds which were heard and the big features of the landscape. Comparing responses can reveal different biases in people's attention.

Writing exercises, as we have already seen, can also be useful in identifying gaps in our perception. A description of a familiar place will demonstrate what was and was not noticed, as well showing something about the way that it was viewed. An exercise which can be used to explore this involves inviting the group members to write for five minutes about a place which they have all visited. They can then look at the discrepancies between different descriptions. Such an exercise can finish with a return to the place itself.

One should be wary of over-interpreting such exercises. There may be quite practical reasons why some things are included in a person's description and others are excluded. Not only will people's patterns of perception vary, but also there may be differences in their experiences of being in the space. Where the person was standing or sitting when they visited the place and what they did there will affect their field of vision and therefore their recollection. Any instructions that were given by the facilitator and form of the exercise itself will also affect recall, sometimes in obvious ways, but sometimes more subtly. For example, when I wrote the description of the yard which appears in the last chapter, I noticed that I had missed out several significant features of the area in my first draft. Reflecting on it afterwards I realised that these features had not actually figured in anyone's activity during the exercise, so that, although they were in my general 'mental map' of the yard, they were not in my specific one related to the exercise.

Such observations are useful in helping us to guard against over interpretation. There is always a danger of group members, or facilitators, engaging in a sort of quasi-psychoanalysis based on rather dubious data of this kind. Nevertheless such exercises do reveal that there is more than one way to see a place, and that perception is influenced by personal phenomena. Particularly they reveal the shortcomings of memory. Our memories of places and events can involve shocking distortions or omissions. Such a discovery can have sobering repercussions for therapy in general.

Not all attractive phenomena are problematic though. We often have a healthy intuition of what will be nourishing and supportive to us. We are drawn to things which will lead us towards new, creative insights. We are caught by things which interest us because they are interesting and because they inspire us. Part of the attraction of working with the natural world is the way that it surrounds us with beauty and positive images of growth and fruition. When we experience the environment we encounter phenomena which are real. Our senses may be selective and sometimes distorting, but they are the windows through which we meet our surroundings. The experience of meeting these things draws us towards health.

So, whilst we can analyse the processes of attraction and aversion, however imperfect our perception is, it is ultimately founded on perception of reality, and that reality is the source of our psychological and spiritual health.

During our summer programme, we used a walking exercise similar to that described above to explore participants' experiences of attraction and aversion. As they walked through an area of woodland, the group members were invited to observe the way that their minds were drawn to some things and reacted against others. Afterwards they sat and reflected on the process individually.

This sort of simple exercise is not unlike the process of insight meditation, where the constantly changing activity of the mind is observed with as neutral an attitude as possible. It benefits from taking place in a context where the mind is caught by real objects and can be surprised by the unexpected, rather than simply regenerating its habitual patterns of thought.

The mind is constantly following the eye and ear and the other senses, engaging with things in a self-interested way. Meditation of this kind is practised with the intention of unhooking reactivity by not allowing it to get a hold. We cannot stop the mind's initial impulse towards the object but we can abort the process of attachment by observing it instead of acting on it. If we use the meditative attitude to regard the natural world, the environment becomes a mirror to our conditioned mentality, and also reveals some of the sources of anxiety and fear which lead to its formation. Then natural phenomena will speak to us, offering constant reminders of their real existence, and waking us out of the sluggish cycles of mental activity in which we get hooked again and again by the mind's old scripts.

Chapter Eleven

The Fire Element

We are making a fire today. David and I are clearing the space under the overhead electricity cables. Earlier this year Electricité de France came through our land with their big machine and cut a swathe through the hazels and field-maples which have grown up beneath their power line, leaving a thicket of brambles and stumps and broken branches. This last happened ten years ago and will no doubt happen again on a similar cycle if we do not keep the land cleared ourselves. We do not really mind for it would have been a huge amount of work to have coppiced the whole stretch where the line crosses our woods; the equivalent of two field lengths. At the same time, we would love to keep the access to the area at the far end of the line, which will become overgrown and inaccessible once more if the bushes grow up again. Clearing the remaining debris from the ground it is not easy though, for the old stumps regenerate quickly and our small brush cutting machine hits up against them as we try to make a path through, often suffering injury as a result and requiring yet another visit to the repair shop. So we today are burning out stumps.

There is plenty of dead wood that is not good enough to saw into logs for winter with which we can make the bonfires. It is thin brushwood and much of it is twisted and broken by the cutting machine. We collect it and pile it over a dead stump at the opening to the cutting. We also get dry grass from the hay field as tinder. The grass was cut earlier in the summer and is lying on the ground. I stuff some of this under the mound of twigs as kindling.

Burning fires at the edge of a hay field requires care. Too

large or furious and a spark could ignite a conflagration that could sweep through a large area out of control. The oak wood too is dry, and the floor of leaf mould and twigs could easily take light. The power cables themselves are well above the flames but too much heat could melt the insulation. So we light fires with care.

Perhaps the risk is part of the attraction. We crave an edge of danger, and the possibility of losing control. It is strange how humans like to court such thrills. The moment when the first rush of flame bursts through the grass, crackling and sparking, is one of pure exhilaration. Then there comes that tinge of anxiety. Will the small twigs catch light before the transient passion of this initial burning fades, leaving the remains of the hay as a smoking tangled mat of blackened ashes? Will the thin, easy to burn twigs go up in flames too quickly or will they burn long enough to ignite the bigger sticks before their energy is spent? The fire establishes itself through a chain. Tinder gives light to twigs, which in turn give light to bigger wood. Then it would be possible to add logs if we wanted to. With each stage, burning becomes more sustained and the flames more established. Otherwise the fire dies, leaving a few twigs reduced to smouldering fragments, red embers dropping into bare unreceptive earth beneath the unscathed heap of dead wood.

So today we have created a bonfire with a particular structure, designed to catch easily so that it will quickly become controllable. There is grass at the bottom, small twigs and then larger ones on top. Order before chaos; we arrange the timbers so that the flames will embrace them fast and efficiently.

I strike a match. The grass burns easily. Only a touch to the wad of stems, and yellow tongues are already darting across the surface of the sun-bleached hay. A breeze catches it and suddenly, with a rushing noise, a burst of heat is sucking the flames through the space beneath the pile of wood which we have built. They are engulfing the whole construction. Dense smoke billows from beneath, clouding up into the blue sky, astringent, brown and flecked with ash and the occasional orange fragment of fire. Small twigs dissolve in sparks and, as they do so, larger ones begin to flame and blacken. The fire has caught.

In the early stages, we allow it to flare up, fast and unbounded, for only such free energy can release the wood's potential to burn. Of course we ensure that it is isolated from the obvious places where it could spread, but here it is wild and unpredictable. The fire is vulnerable too. A gust of wind can whip it into flaming activity but, on the other hand, a lull in the breeze or a gust of wind in the wrong direction can lead the flames to drop and falter, like a becalmed kite falling from the sky.

Gradually the transient passion subdues into a more sober burning. Larger branches are alight. We watch, standing back from the heat, but close enough to prevent the fire getting out of control. Occasionally we stamp on a straying lip of flames in the short grass at the edge of the fire patch.

Eventually the red glow of embers replaces the initial burst of flame, and what remains of the wood is charred into cracked blackened tree forms and white ashes. The first pile of wood is now nearly eliminated, consumed by the rush of the fire. A few larger logs continue to smoulder on. We throw on more sticks, feeding the fire, encouraging it to eat deep into the knotted wood of the stump, a thick lump, deformed by past cutting and regrowth. We will it to blacken and crumble in the flames.

As the first stump is burned away, we encourage the fire to move on to the next. By adding sticks to one side of the fire, we edge the flames towards the second stump, which is a yard or two to the right of the first. The wood chippings on the ground, left by the electricity company's machine, ignite of their own accord and we add to them from the brushwood that lies in the undergrowth nearby. There are oak branches, twisted and gnarled and covered in lichen, too small to take back to the house, fallen from the trees of the wood in long past storms. Also pieces of straight hazel stem, smooth barked and easily broken. Sometimes we use these in the garden, but they are better cut fresh. Dead wood is not so strong, already decaying internally due to the fungi and bugs which have infiltrated it. With the bill hook we drag cut thistles into the flames, avoiding touching them lest the near invisible thorns embed themselves in our fingers.

With each addition the fire bursts into renewed vigour. Sometimes it flares up immediately as dried up weeds from the field combust in seconds. Other times it takes longer, minutes of patience, waiting for the fresh sticks to ignite, waiting for the wind to deliver the extra oxygen necessary to whip a smouldering branch back into life.

Fire has a fascination. The draw of the bonfire with its dark smoky scent and crackling heat is irresistible. In part the incipient danger, but perhaps more the creativity of the process of destruction, lures us. We feed more and more prunings and garden debris into the flames. In a moment of glory we see the fruits of our efforts expand into a sky-high sheet of energy as the fire rushes up towards the heavens. But then it dies back, craving resuscitation. Caught by the excitement, we gather more offerings of sticks and branches. We become slaves to its hunger, searching for every scrap of rubbish that it can devour. We are tempted by the glory. Prometheus-like we steal for a moment the passion of the gods and attempt to harness it, to ride the dragon of its destructiveness.

There is a cleansing process, a purging, in reducing a pile of dishevelled forest cuttings to bare blackened earth and a few charred bits of wood.

After I wrote the previous section, I shared it on our community's interactive website. A member in Australia, Robert

McCarthy, responded to my writing, reminding me that, for people over there, wild fires are an everyday fear. It is easy for those of us living in wetter countries to forget just how destructive such fires can be. Although in Britain acres of moorland can be burned by heath fires, it is rare for much lasting damage to be done. Indeed, swaling, the deliberate burning of heather and bracken on the moors, has long been practised in our country.

Last year terrible fires swept through Kingslake, an area in which Robert used to live. After the fires had been extinguished, he revisited the area to see for himself the destruction, and meet the community he knew and loved. He found his old friends in a state of shock, surrounded by devastation and the remnants of what had once been their communal buildings and homes.

Receiving his message, I asked if he would write about his experience of revisiting and he responded:

Fire reduces whatever it touches to simpler forms. This fire reduced everything to black and white, charcoal and ash. The closest details now just textures; the distant mountain ridges and gullies, colour stolen by flame. The treasured lush undergrowth of giant tree ferns, mosses, blackwood, silver wattle, banksia; all reduced to a deep white ash dressing for the naked, scorched earth. The giants of the forest; messmate, mountain ash, mountain grey gum, stringybarks, now just an assortment of black lifeless stumps strewn at many angles, some still smouldering. A landscape suddenly featureless, freed from time.

And the bush is silenced, nothing stirs, shocked into stillness. Even conversations are so strained. What can be said? Stories are just starting to form. More than twenty of my friends' neighbours died, human remains remain in the ashes. Our eyes get drawn to some shiny, frozen puddles, car engines that had flowed. And the familiar smells of the damp mosses, the eucalyptus, the wattle; gone. Only the harsh smell of charcoal permeates all. As the sadness permeates all.

Suddenly a lyre bird runs past. "Must have survived in a wombat hole," someone ecstatically exclaims. These birds always bring joy in their sudden appearance, in normal times. This moment's joy brings a moment's colour. A light so intense we look away. The community has an annual midwinter census of this wonderful bird. Many people stand in the forest in the dawn chill recording the birds' calls. So our minds moved to how this year's survey would be. But it is much too early to look to any future. Not yet.

Fire is one of the elements upon which early Buddhists meditated. As with the other elements, it is experienced both in the forms we encounter in the world and in our bodies. In meditation we explore these parallels, the fire within and the fire without.

The fire element exists in our body as heat. Whilst we live, our bodies are warm. We are indeed, warm-blooded creatures, burning the calories which we consume as fuel in order to maintain our body temperature at a constant 36 degrees centigrade. When we are sick, our temperature may rise just a little, as the body tries to discomfort and eliminate invading bacteria or viruses by becoming feverish, but it is a delicate balance, for too great a rise in temperature disrupts the mechanisms of various key organs, including the brain, sending us, in the extreme, into fitting or coma states.

When we die, on the other hand, we get cold. The metabolic processes which create heat cease and our inner fire goes out. The warmth leaves the body. It becomes a corpse and the process of decay sets it. We merge back into the earth.

Preserving body temperature is an essential and sometimes challenging task for humans. Our bodies shiver and raise mats of hair, creating goose-bumps, but we do not have the thick coats of fur like other animals which can be raised to trap a layer of air. We cannot fluff up our feathers as birds do on cold winter mornings, nor can we hibernate, our tails wrapped around us as comforters, like dormice do. Instead we clothe ourselves, piling on jumpers, coats, hats, scarves and gloves on winter mornings.

Some adaptation happens naturally as the body adjusts to new conditions. Often when we first arrive in France in winter, the house seems cold and uncomfortable in comparison with being in a centrally heated house in England. After a few days we adjust. Then, when we return to urban life, the houses seem far too hot and we go round opening windows and turning off radiators. Likewise in summer, at first the heat can seem overwhelming when we arrive, but we soon get used to it and stop noticing the difference. Within certain margins, the body accommodates the changes and adjusts its internal thermostat.

Hormones affect our response to temperature too. Menopausal women throw cardigans on and off and fling open windows idiosyncratically as their bodies, for little apparent reason, decide to change temperature and overheat. Hot flushes can range from bothersome to paralysing. In the daytime they can leave one sweating and flustered at one moment, and turning up the heating the next. At night they disrupt sleep, leaving husbands who are brave enough to still occupy the same bed bemused or irritated as the shared duvet is thrown off one minute and reclaimed the next and windows are flung open or closed.

Pregnancy too can leave a woman feeling overheated. The combination of hormones and a greater body bulk changes one's relationship to temperature completely. When I was expecting my first baby and in the later stages of pregnancy, even in a chilly March, I rarely wore a coat out of doors. My baby and my body gave me all the warmth I needed. A stocky mushroom of a figure, I would waddle round our town centre in short-sleeved T-shirts amid the other shoppers, carrying a micro-climate of my own, whilst they huddled themselves up in winter coats.

So fire can be a physical element in our bodies.

Fire can also be perceived in psychological processes. It is common to think of certain emotions as fiery. We speak of people being hot-tempered, or hot with passion. Anger and lust are both thus associated with heat. They are the emotions which consume us, which involve us. Unlike the cool emotions, which generally involve withdrawal from others, these hot emotions engage us in strong encounters, whether friendly or otherwise. Fervent, impatient, overbearing, they force themselves upon us and on those around us with vigour.

In fact, the physical and the emotional are not really separate. Hot emotional states often also involve real bodily changes. They generate heat both physically and metaphorically. This is probably why they are so called. Anger creates a reddened face and burning palms, raising the body temperature and causing a rush of blood to the head. Passion raises the temperature in other ways, warming our hearts and our genitals, swelling those intimate areas which crave sexual satisfaction with the heat of expectation. Other emotions change our body temperature. Anxiety quickens the pulse and makes us sweat. Embarrassment makes us blush, red-faced. Fear chills us and brings us out in cold sweats. Excitement warms us.

Food tastes so much better cooked on an open fire. There is something illogical about the enjoyment that comes from eating baked beans tinged with the taste of wood smoke, ash flecked sausages and roast potatoes charred on one side, but still it is one of the culinary delights I fondly remember from childhood. Porridge brewed up in a huge cauldron on a slow fire and slightly burned on the bottom has a taste so subtle that it can never be reproduced in a regular kitchen and the steaming kettle on the old metal tripod amid the smoke of the campfire is one of the most welcoming sights I know first thing in the morning.

Today we are cooking dinner at the fire circle. The group has divided into fire-lighters and foragers. The fire lighting group has collected a good heap of dry sticks from the nearby woods, piling them up at the edge of the circle. The foragers have been to the kitchen and assembled a collection of provisions and some pans that we can use on an open fire with the help of Sumaya, who is on cooking duty for the community.

I am helping the fire team. By the time we have the wood assembled and the fire built, the foragers are chopping onions into the stew pan. Campfire cooking is usually best kept a simple matter, and they have opted for adding jars of ready cooked chick peas and tins of tomatoes mixed with spices to make a base for the stew. There are other vegetables too. We have home-grown courgettes, carrots and beetroot. Someone has already prepared big slices of courgette and aubergine, dipped in oil and sprinkled with herbs and chilli powder ready for barbecuing.

The fire is soon blazing. Once again, we use dry grass to start it and the flames rush away beneath the pile of sticks, catching alight the smallest twigs, which we put at the bottom. Building a campfire is a matter of creating a compact structure in which air can circulate. You put the tinder underneath and then layers of twigs, followed by sticks, increasing in size as you add more layers. You can include reasonably sized sticks on the top – big enough not to burn out in the first few minutes, but you need the smaller sticks to be burning first before these will catch light.

The fire place is a circular heap of stones in the middle of the field, which are mounded on either side to create a central channel. It is in this channel that the fire is built. The fire is constructed by placing a stick transversely across between the two piles of stones that form the sides of the channel, and then leaning the rest of the sticks against it in such a way as to create a sort of funnel which is directed to catch the wind so that the air circulation will help to breathe the reluctant fire into life like natural bellows. The tinder is at the bottom, tucked in from the side so that it can be lit easily.

Today, though, the wind is gusty and fierce, and the fire catches very quickly. We have more concern for it getting out of control. In countries where people cook on fires as a matter of course, it is not uncommon for fires to get out of control and spread to neighbouring buildings. The Great Fire of London started from a baker's cooking fire. Our field is extremely dry, and though we have a cordon of stone and cut ground between the fire and the long dry grass, there is always a risk of sparks flying, especially in the early stages when the fire has to be allowed to roar up in order to catch the wood. I am relieved when we are able to put larger logs on top of the small unpredictable twigs and the fire settles into a steady mix of flame and embers. Nevertheless we have water buckets at the ready just in case.

We have a number of metal grids which can be put across the fire pit to hold the pans, and a heavy iron tripod, donated some years ago by some hippy neighbours before they left town. The grids are mostly old oven shelves, salvaged from cookers destined for the scrap heap. We drop them over the fire so that they rest on the stones on either side. The stew pot goes on one grid, whilst the sliced vegetables are arranged on a barbecue rack on top of the tripod. The fire beneath them is now almost entirely embers, perfect for cooking on.

My namesake, Caroline, is an expert on campfire cooking. She has helped to lead groups in the Australian wilderness, and knows all the tricks to produce a good outdoor meal. She has taken a strong hand in the preparation of the vegetables and her confidence gives others encouragement to join in. Soon the pot of stew is boiling and foil-wrapped potatoes are lying amongst the flickering red embers. The vegetables are browning nicely on the grid. We have only dropped one in the ash, and that was quickly brushed off and returned to the rack. Water is boiling in another pan for couscous.

We eat the meal sitting in a semicircle around the fire pit, the smoke trailing off through the gap that we have left. It tastes very good and there is no shortage of takers for second helpings. Caroline has sliced whole bananas, still in their skins, lengthways and put pieces of chocolate inside each to melt. These are now sitting on the barbecue grid. When the first course is finished, we each have to find a banana buddy with whom to share, because there is only half a one each. The chocolate and banana have melted together into a delicious gooey desert. We find various techniques for sharing it with our partners.

When we have finished eating, we relax around the remains of the fire. The washing up will need to be carried back and done on the table outside the house, so there is nothing immediate to do but watch the fire gradually transform itself into a heap of white and grey ashes, still tinged with dull red embers, glowing in its core. The sun is getting low in the sky and we throw on more wood for a last burst of flame before departing back along the path through the field.

One of the Buddha's best known talks is known as The Fire Sermon.[28] This teaching was the third ever taught by the Buddha after his enlightenment. In it the Buddha talks about how all the senses are on fire. We are aflame with greed, hatred and confusion, the three modes of attachment. These passionate impulses of attraction and aversion permeate our sense bases, the uncontrollable organs of perception. Through such impulses we are constantly drawn into relationship and fascination with the various objects of our desire or revulsion which we come across in the world.

In other words, as each of the senses locks onto its objects, the things to which it gives attention, old habit energies are activated. We hook onto our habitual attachments because our senses are always on the lookout for opportunities and associations on which to build the sense of continuity and security which we identify with. We enjoy the sight of things which fascinate, tempt, flatter or disgust us because they support our world view. As a result we are pulled into the cycle of reaction and reinforcement which ties us into all the unhealthy, habitual processes of the unenlightened mind. The process of self-creation rests on fiery, passion-filled, attachment.

The Buddha used the metaphor of fire. Fire is both dangerous and fascinating. It attracts us through its energy and can be useful in providing heat or cooking, but if we are not careful, it burns us. So in the Fire Sermon, the point which is being made is that it is all too easy to get inflamed by things of the world. There is spiritual danger everywhere in the form of temptations and provocations. It is all too easy for us to become angry or covetous, lustful or jealous. Guarding against this fire, we protect ourselves from getting carried away in our emotional reactions.

The metaphor of fire is not only found in the Fire Sermon. It also pervades many of the other teachings, a recurring image of the dangerous passions, and the enlightened state is often equated to a cooling of the passions.

In *The Feeling Buddha*,[29] however, David Brazier writes of the third Noble Truth, *Nirodha*, suggesting that the image which the Buddha is alluding to by choosing this word is of the embankment which is created around a cooking fire. A mud wall is often created around the fire pit in order to shelter it from the wind and make the fire useable, rather as we surround our campfire with a mound of stones. It prevents the fire getting out of control, but does not extinguish it. Indeed it concentrates it, making its energy stronger.

So, rather than suggesting that we should extinguish our passions, as the teaching is commonly interpreted, this points towards an interpretation of the Buddha's metaphor that suggests that we can contain the fire of our spiritual passions and harness them towards our spiritual journey.

Our fire is our energy, our capacity for growth. It enables us to engage with the important things in our lives. It is the spiritual force which allows us to live effectively. Like fire, the passionate energy of attraction which we feel towards the world of objects has both the potential to engage us with others, to be useful, and also the danger of getting out of hand and raging through the world uncontained and destructive, creating self-interested agendas and harming others. Our fear of its destructive nature should not, however, dissuade us from allowing our passions to be fully engaged in the process of life. As we watch the fire and guard it to prevent it getting out of hand, so too we can find ways to express ourselves which draw on the energy source within us without letting it take over.

Chapter Twelve

The Water Element

We go to the lake in the evening to swim. The day has been hot and even though the sun is now low in the sky, it is still warm on our bare skin as we change into our swimming costumes on the little sandy beach beneath the pine trees. This place is one which we have been using all summer. We make ourselves at home here on the shore. We are swimming outside the designated swimming area, and there is a frisson of disobedience. As with many French lakes, there are areas for swimming, for boats and for fishing, each separated off by ropes of plastic floats and labelled with big white sign boards. We are in the boating section, but the boat man has long since gone home to dinner and the lake has only few solitary walkers exploring its banks.

It is deliciously silent. I am first to be ready and tread cautiously into the water. The area near the shore has small stones on the bed so unless one is careful in planting the feet, it can be painful. Rather like aquatic animals which lumber awkwardly on land, we stumble out the first few yards, faltering as we find our footholds. Once thigh deep, however, the water is deep enough to swim, and here, with a grateful plunge, I transform, seal-like, into a swimming thing.

Getting one's shoulders under is always a challenge. Here, though, the water is warm as a tepid bath. The shock of cold is brief, a mere contrast to the heat of the air, and a welcome relief after a day of incessant sun. I am swimming immediately, out deep into the water, which is soft textured, smooth and dark as liquid chocolate, with a slight brackishness which comes from the peaty soil of the pine woods.

I swim with a slow and measured breaststroke, not breaking

the surface with arms or feet, preserving the quiet. Willow seeds, light and fluffy as fairies, chase ahead of me, dancing on the breeze across a surface of reflections so clear they are simply an inversion of reality. Pull, breathe, pull, breathe, pull, breathe. My body finds its rhythm without rush or effort. I luxuriate in taking time to cross the hundred yards or so to the other shore of the lake. No need to be anywhere. Just floating, suspended in time and space, by the warm, deep water.

Eventually I arrive. The far side is reeded and the pond bottom is soft with mud and decaying leaves. My feet find hold among the shifting debris. A small trail of bubbles rises to the surface, tickling their way between my toes and releasing cloudings of brown mud into the water. I stand looking back, watching the heads of the others spread out across the width of the lake.

Here the sun is behind me. Its golden evening light catches the red trunks of the trees on the bank whence we have come. Grey-green canopies create a skyline against the deep summer blue. Everything is bright, details etched by the crisp light. The water is smooth, but for the wake left by the swimmers. Behind me, in the reeds, small birds fidget and chatter. Overhead a rook is circling. Or maybe it is a crow. Beyond this, though, all is silent.

The others arrive and we stand a while chatting companionably, neck deep in the water. Nothing moves except the birds and the occasional splash from a fish, jumping to catch one of the midges that skim the water and sending concentric rings of ripples out across the mirrored surface. We watch, relaxing our eyes on the nothingness of evening. Absence of needs, absence of concerns, absence of thoughts, minds subsiding into the stillness of the water, glassy and transparent.

Then we are swimming back in slow leisured sweeping strokes, each ending in a pause like the space between breaths. I glide back through the warm, treacled water, back towards the trees, the beach and our discarded clothes. The sun is setting now, sinking down behind the trees, far across the main body of the lake. It tinges the sky orange and pink, casting the low lines of cloud into purple shadows. The water is even calmer. Night is on its way. Not a movement. Sky and reflection meet at the tree line.

One day when we swam here we saw a snake swimming in the water. It was quite close by. It swam an arc, away from the land, on the near side where we changed, and curving in towards the shore a little way off, to disappear in among another reed bed further up the shore. Perhaps it was looking for young birds. Its head stood out, proud, from the surface of the lake, and its body beneath the water left a bow wave. It did not seem to mind us, for we were not far off, but it waited till we had left the water before returning to its home by retracing its track.

Other times we saw small fishes, swimming in shoals, flying right out of the water. The tiny bodies, only an inch or two long, flashed silver as they caught the light, but when we peered into the shallows to which they had returned the fish were tiny brown creatures, and quite different from the silver flying darts they had been in air. Sometimes they stayed around and nibbled at our feet as we paddled there. Mostly they swam away, fast as they arrived.

Swimming in the lake is one of the most peaceful activities I know. After a hot day working in the garden or running an event, an evening swim creates a breathing space, a transition that eases day into night. The water is spacious. Unlike a swimming pool, it merges into the landscape. Its boundaries are wide and indistinct. Muddy margins or banks of rushes fade land into water and water into land. The reflected sky seems simply a continuation of its captured light. In such freedom the body relaxes. Warm air slows activity. Lulled into somnolence, time becomes irrelevant. Immediacy of experience intensifies as the world recedes.

The body moves as one organism, arms and legs in co-ordination. Held by the water, the forces of gravity no longer seem to play. We float, supported, surrounded; embraced. Morphing into fishlike beings we undulate with water flowing over us, under us, through us. Taking refuge in water we ourselves melt into fluidity and become as one with our surroundings.

I wake in the night to the sound of rain on my tent. The rhythmic pit pat is insistent enough to drag me out of a deep dream and I take moments to remember where I am. I lie, catching the sound, drifting sleepily through layers of consciousness. It is warm and I have thrown off some of my covers. I snuggle back into them and enjoy the softness of their billowiness, like clouds of thistledown, blowing across the field.

The raindrops are intensifying. They come harder and faster. There is something compelling about the sound, but something relaxing too. Like a heartbeat it soothes me in the womb of my sleeping bag. There are few pleasures in life that equal lying in a tent in the rain and not having to get up.

The prospect of getting up, of course, raises different emotions. Emerging from the tent into the stinging cold of rain shafts, or discovering that water has penetrated the nylon shell and stands in dark unwelcoming puddles on the groundsheet at the entrance, or, worse, in my shoes, left too close to the fabric the night before, has far less comforting effect.

But tonight there are still hours of sleep to be had and the rain clouds may well have rolled on eastward by morning. So I lie, enjoying the warmth and the staccato sound of falling drops.

We are born out of water. When we enter this world we have already lain for nine months in an aquatic haven, rocked and soothed by the movement of our mother's life. We have listened to the sounds of her inner world: the thud of her pumping heart, the gurgle and swish of intestinal meanderings, the circulation of blood in tissue. All water sounds. Her body is composed of water, infused by water and served by water. A bag of liquids, if punctured it bleeds.

Our early movements are swimming. Limbs extend and stretch through the amniotic lake as we kick out and discover our muscularity. Our mouth gulps fluid as we suck fingers and thumbs and practise feeding. We are nourished by liquid. The blood that flows from the placenta carries all we need and all we receive. Even after birth, we continue to be fed by liquid, a flowing ongoing connection to our mother's body, sensuous and comforting.

So I doze into primeval sleep, soothed by the pattering on the skin of my tent.

It is raining when we go to the bamboo grove to meditate. Light rain has been falling on and off all morning and Massimo warns us to be prepared to sit in the rain. Some people bring thick jackets and even umbrellas but I decide that, as it is summer, I will risk a more minimal approach. Exploring the environment, I reflect, cannot be a fair weather pastime. Rain too is an aspect of the real encounter. I put on a sleeveless body warmer, padded and thick to keep my core temperature up, but beneath it I have only very light cotton trousers and a cotton shirt.

Walking into the grove I feel a mix of interest and resistance. There is a fine drizzle and I wonder if the bamboo will provide any protection. Passing the barn, I pick up a piece of polystyrene, thick and rectangular and just the right size for a meditation cushion. I find my place and sit down.

Soon drops of water are landing on my head and arms. I see the cloth of my trousers scattered with a growing number of round patches as the water creates spots on the dry fabric. Thoughts run through my head. The rain is increasing. Spots appear more frequently and start to join up. Soon my trousers will be soaked. How long will it be before my jacket also becomes water-logged? Will I get too wet and cold by sitting through this session and end up sick? I am aware that I have a tendency to be affected by temperature changes so this is not an idle thought. Several times when I was younger I got mild exposure when I was involved in outdoor activities and got chilled. I learned to be careful. Is my idea of experiencing the rain just a romantic notion?

On the other hand, I reflect, this is still summer, and, although the day is not as warm as some have been recently, it is certainly not cold either. I question my resistance. If this were water in the lake or from a shower, I would not be avoiding it. Of course, sitting still does carry a risk of chilling, but at least at present the sensation of water dripping on my body is not actually unpleasant when I stop fighting it and relax.

Drops continue falling on my knees, my shoulders, and my head. They touch lightly, like fingers tapping me. I sit, letting them arrive, observing the pattern they make.

The rain is increasing. It comes in waves, slowing to a scattering of droplets then arriving with renewed force as a gust of wind drives the clouds across the sky. When each showering arrives, I hear the first flurry of water as it first hits the far side of the bamboo clump. Wind and rain lash the leaves some moments before they arrive at my sitting spot. I hear them gradually sweep across the patch, arriving at last as large heavy drops that fall around me and over me. I am protected from the wind, but hear it in the leaves above me. The rain, on the other hand, gets through.

The drops on my legs meet up and water drips through the material of my trousers onto the ground. I am getting soaked. I notice once more my tendency to tense against the wet, but then remember to find my curiosity and relax. I am warm enough in my body warmer and the rain has not penetrated it yet. Even if my legs are wet and a little cold it is fine. I am grateful for the polystyrene block which forms my seat, surprised by how much warmth it seems to generate. I sit, enjoying the musical rhythm on falling drops.

A fortnight after the eco-therapy week, I go to visit my friends in The Hague. They live not too far from the beach, so Leo invites me to go swimming in the sea with him whilst Annetta is helping a friend to prepare for a community event. It is grey today, the sky heavy with clouds which threaten rain, but the air is warm and muggy still. It will be good to swim after my long drive yesterday.

We take the car a couple of kilometres towards the sea and find a space to park in the road that runs along behind the dunes. There is a cycle track with a pathway beside it leading through the dunes towards the beach. The dunes are Holland's defence, Leo says. The Dutch care for them, knowing their importance to their country. Without them their country would return to an uninhabitable swamp.

The path climbs a slight rise as it enters the sandy ridge of the dunes. To begin with the area is wooded. Trees arch over the gravel track. A number of people are out walking. We pass through an area of sycamores, surprising for their proximity to the sea. The trees are short, half the size of inland trees of the same variety, often with multiple trunks which grow and branch into strange sculptural forms. The wood is beautiful, and slightly eerie. Gradually though, these stunted trees give way to open sandy ground, anchored by grass and rough dune-land scrub and traversed by other paths. Here the track itself has become sandy, and there are duckboards on the upward slopes, making walking easier.

Over the last rise we see the sea, a grey expanse, stretching out to a horizon where it meets the grey sky. Grey on grey in every subtle shade. The wind here is stronger and the waves, flecked up into white crests, look uninviting. The sandy beach extends in either direction and, to our right in the distance, terminates in a stone breakwater of a small harbour. People sit in a beach café, a cheery summer house of a building, constructed of timber and glass, and perched above the tideline. They drink lattes from tall glasses and watch young men performing stunts on their ski-boards, propelled by kites that billow and strain in the wind.

On the horizon a row of hulls, empty container ships at anchor, await berths in the great ports of Rotterdam and Hook of Holland. Closer at hand, small sailing dinghies are putting out into the breakers. People in jackets and fleeces walk dogs along the tideline. A couple of figures are surfing in wetsuits, riding their boards on the large, driving waves, but no one else is in the sea.

Finding a spot, high up on the beach beyond the café, we disrobe. It is an act of faith, but in fact the wind is not cold. I stand, looking out to sea as Leo finishes changing, then, leaving our small piles of clothing on the sand, we run down to the sea.

The first contact with the water is a shock of cold. As my feet and ankles sink into the wet sand, there is a moment of doubt, for the water is far chillier than the air, but I am in.

The sea is restless and unrelenting and does not allow for gradual entry. Wave on wave breaks further up the legs as I edge my way forwards. We wade into them, bracing ourselves against their blows, greeting their force with our bodies.

"Do not go too deep," Leo says.

But there is no need for warning. Both of us have grown up with the sea and tales of drownings. We know to respect the currents and not go beyond our depths. The undertow can drag you out. Watch out for the out-tide.

Whilst swimming in a lake can be quiet and meditative, swimming in the sea is energising and vigorous. I am soon chest deep in the water, but the depth of the sea is a constantly changing process, for the waves never cease their churning motion, rising and falling as they advance, and sometimes my feet leave the seabed as I try to keep my face above the surface. The wind is coming on shore, driving the North Sea breakers towards the beach. Great walls of water rise ahead of me, their crests breaking into a foaming turmoil as they arch over, enveloping the in-between space before descending, crashing over my head. I remember as a child loving to get caught in that secret world, that magical glassy tunnel beneath the curling wave crest, completely encircled by the water, yet in the air. For a moment separated from everything else in the world by my private bubble of water before being plunged, spluttering and smarting into the salty surge of sea water.

I leap up into the heaving water, letting myself be lifted by the waves' strength, my body held in the grasp of their motion. There is nothing to do but surrender to their unrelenting power as they sweep in towards the beach. Nothing, except to jump and rise and fall. We shout and laugh as we are tossed, human flotsam, on the rolling water.

When we stand on the earth, we are aware of its solidity. We feel the reliability of the ground, an unchanging constant presence. Refuge in water is quite unlike refuge in earth. Water holds us intimately. We are clasped, held, immersed, supported, lifted, completely at the will of the element. It caresses and surrounds every part of our body as we swim in it. Sometimes we float. It always seems a little strange that we, heavy embodied creatures that we are, can be supported on the surface of water. Other times we sink, plunged deep into the torrent, only to be released, bobbing like corks to the surface.

Learning to swim involves learning to trust, to develop faith, to release our belief that we must do all ourselves and that nothing is reliable beyond our personal power of effect. We must trust the water and allow ourselves to be held by it, not resting on it as we do on the land, but immersing ourselves in it, cradled by it, within it yet not a part of it, floating on the surface, yet half enfolded. In water we are not still. Water is always moving, and we move with it to stay afloat. It is a partnership, a passionate engagement. On earth we direct our movements, but in water, and particularly in the sea, we are moved whether we will it or not. As with a lover, we learn to anticipate, to flow, to submit to its power.

Eventually we have had enough. Although the August sea has been warmed by a summer of sun, the wind and cloud make it cold for swimming too long. Leo goes first and I follow, letting the waves wash me back towards the shore until I am obliged to stand, knee deep in the water. We climb the beach and retrieve our clothes, the salt drying on our goose-fleshed skin as we rub ourselves down.

We drink a coffee in the café, watching the sea from the slatted wood deck. The water is in constant motion, dappling, shifting shades of grey and mauve and green and brown. The lads on ski-boards jump high into the air, twirling their boards above their heads, and splashing down again into the waves before regaining their balance. Further out, the sailboats cluster round the instructors' launches, as youngsters learn to manage them. There are no swimmers now, except a solitary dog further up the shore.

Chapter Thirteen

Dark Spaces

It has not been an easy meeting of the community. The group have been discussing various contentious issues and feelings were sometimes raised. I am conscious of regrets about some of the things I have said myself, and also that I did not respond better to others. Even though there has been some useful resolution and I know the bad feelings will be resolved with time and more conversations, the atmosphere feels heavy as I leave the room. I need space to reflect and let go.

I walk out of the building to go to my tent. It is late and the sun set some time ago. After the light of the house, the darkness feels intense. There is something inviting about it. I do not feel ready for sleep. My mind is still racing. I am tempted to go and sit for a while in the meditation hall. It is peaceful, and I love the way that it is open to the air and to the night. There I will be able to gather my thoughts and let myself settle through some meditative practice. Sitting in the old stone building, perhaps with the mellow light of a single candle, one can feel oneself settling, finding refuge, and giving space for the experiences to be digested. At the end of the day it can be quite magical there with the flickering light, the shifting interplay of shadows, the subtle scent of incense, and the sound of bats flying in and out, sweeping the air above my head for insects.

As I walk across the yard, however, I see a bright half-moon emerging from behind the barn, floating high in the sky, yellow-white against the night. The air is crisp and sharp, already chilled. Stars are visible overhead, pinpricks of light but, ahead of me, their light is obscured by the greater brilliance of the moon.

The thought comes to me that, rather than going to the shrine, I could be out in the moonlight. Moonlight is associated with the Chinese Buddhist figure, Quan Yin, a female Buddha who represents compassion. We sometimes chant to her out of doors on full moon nights. In fact the moon is significant in several Buddhist schools, and many festivals and practices are timed by lunar calendars. Not only Buddhism. In other religious traditions the moon also takes on significance. There is something about the cool bright light which speaks to the spirit in all of us, and the ancients, without street lights or indoor lives, felt guided and comforted by its clarity, their lives organised by its rhythmic changes. It is pre-religious, a primitive association which is ground into our being at a cellular level. Dark phases alternate with nights so bright that the traveller can follow a path with ease. Always changing yet predictable, the light wanes over weeks until it fades completely, only to return, a fine, sweet crescent of hope and a promise of the new. It is a cycle echoed in the tides and in women's bodies, our watery homage to our powerful Lady of the Night.

Seeing the bright quarter moon, my feeling is visceral, instinctive. The pale, sharp light and the freshness of the air evoke a state of reverence. I want to be outside, bathed in the other-worldly luminosity. I want to sit in the spaciousness, to connect with the beauty of the night. I want to be touched by the silence and feel it seep into my troubled thoughts, letting the turmoil settle, like leaves fluttering down to the ground after a storm. I want the calm, clear moonlight to enfold me like a child, soothing me back to tranquillity. So it is that I head for the bamboo grove.

As I walk across the field, I imagine that the moonlight, filtering through the filigree of the bamboo leaves, will enhance the atmosphere of the space. I feel my way along the path carefully, testing each footstep as I place it. I cannot see my feet, but I know roughly where the path goes, and the well worn channel of cut grass that winds through the garden and across the rough of the field guides me. Dew is falling and I smell the wetness of the cut hay and the acrid scent of the elder plants at the edge of the patch, clear and cold in my nostrils.

The path gets darker as it goes into the bamboo. The clump is so thick that as I enter it I cannot see any glimmer of light ahead of me. Although I am familiar with the path, in this complete darkness I am lost, reliant on other senses to find my way. I reach out in front of me. My outstretched hands meet bamboo canes, smooth, tall and hard. They guide me in finding the spaces between the stems as the path winds and twists. I know that the moon is in the direction towards which I am walking, on the far side of the patch, and that the path will bend round and run parallel with the hedge on that side. For the present, though, I am walking in complete darkness, slowly and carefully feeling my way along.

When I reach the turn in the path, a little moonlight is filtering through between the canes. I am surprised by how little light is in fact getting through. I had expected a clear sight of the moon in the spaces between the canes, imagining the bamboo leaves and stems in silhouette against the silver-white disc, like a Japanese print. In fact only a very faint lightening of the space ahead can be seen as the canes are more densely packed than I had expected.

It is only when I come to the far side of the grove that I can actually see the moon, classically placed behind a few straight canes, their delicate tracery of leaves forming black shadows across the light. The path is breaking out into the field again, crossing the drainage ditch with its rough stones and the uneven clods of clay between. I do not want to continue on this unpredictable surface in the darkness and, besides, I have come here to experience being in the bamboo at night. So I stand, watching the moon through these last few straggling stems and listening to the noises of the night breaking into the silence.

Cicadas are still chirruping in the field, their tone lower than the grasshoppers, and more melodious. Otherwise the air is still.

I start to walk back into the bamboo. Returning to the darkness, I once more become reliant on my arms held out in front of me to guide me between the stems. I walk slowly, tentatively sweeping the air for obstacles. The way should be familiar as I am retracing my steps, but this time I take a wrong turn, missing a bend in the path, and find myself faced with a wall of canes with no way through. The confusion only lasts a moment, for I soon realise my mistake, but in that moment I am overwhelmed by a rush of feelings. All I can find is the cold, hard tangle of stems. I am filled with a sense of impossibility. There is no way forwards. An image flashes through my mind of being lost in the forest of canes till daybreak. I become simultaneously aware of one thought impulse telling me to give up trying to find a way through and remain trapped in the maze of stems forever and a second which knows that there is no choice but to find a way through regardless of the effort it takes. For a split second I stand, torn between these two impulses.

Of course, at this point, rationality replaces the instinctive drives of struggle and flight; persistence and defeat. I discover the turn in the path that puts me back on the correct track. Soon I am feeling my way back through the darkest area of the clump, hands encountering the canes to either side, checking my progress. Soon I am emerging into the field and the moonlight.

My mind feels calmer. The peace of the night is indeed penetrating my thoughts and though I still mull my earlier words and feel a pang of shame, my orientation is now more towards the future, reflecting on whether there is a need to make amends and vowing to notice earlier if these old patterns of hot responses surface again.

In the small drama of my passage through the canes in the darkness, something has been enacted, something changed. I found myself lost in a maze of unseen barriers, in danger of losing my path and ending up in the interstices of the clump, without direction or a way out. I persisted, despite my urge to give up, and found my way out of the potential trap. Although only momentary, the sequence of journey, trial, impossibility, persistence and resolution mirrored a psychological reality. In an embodied way, I have created a reflection of my mental turmoil; a metaphor for the quagmire of frustration and regret which comes from hitting up against old unhelpful patterns of being. I have found a way through it.

Such experiences are both metaphoric and real. At one level, the challenge of finding my way in the dark is real, focusing mind and body in an unfamiliar situation. Facing challenges creates courage and resilience and although this challenge was relatively minor, it still evoked moments of raw emotion. In challenging situations we extend our capacity to withstand and even enjoy the unforeseen. We discover that what seems to be an insuperable barrier often turns out to be less rigid than it appeared.

At another level, the natural world provided a mirror to the mental confusion which brought me out tonight. In my troubled mind-state, I have been given an experience in which the forest of thoughts which crowd my mind and the unseen morass of conditioned karmic associations have been reflected in a physical way by the real environment. The experience of facing it gives me glimpses of my habitual reactions. It reminds me that I have the capacity to give up when faced with such daunting circumstances. It also reminds me that, with persistence and faith, I can find my way out. Walking in the dark I gain confidence, not just in my body's capacity to use new senses, but also in the fact that a path often exists even when I cannot see it.

The Majjhima Nikaya is one of the books in the Pali Canon. This collection of Buddhist texts contains many accounts of occasions when the Buddha gave teachings to his followers. In this collection there is one text, or sutta,[30] which describes the Buddha talking about his own experience of confronting the fears that arose in him when practising in the forest after dark.

This text describes an occasion when the Buddha is visited by a Brahmin, a member of the priestly class of India. In a way this sutta can be seen as a sort of professional consultation, for the man is coming to ask the Buddha's advice as a fellow teacher. He talks to the Buddha about how he, as a priest, is seen as an example by many people. They have expectations of him and look to him to live a holy life. Yet, he says, he still feels fear when he goes into the depths of the forest. He says:

It's not easy to endure isolated forest or wilderness dwellings. It's not easy to maintain seclusion, not easy to enjoy being alone. The forests, as it were, plunder the mind of a monk who has not attained concentration.[31]

The Buddha agrees with him that overcoming such fear is indeed difficult, and responds by sharing an account of how he, prior to his enlightenment, had similar fears. He describes how he tried to overcome these fears. Firstly he reflected on the possible origins of the fear, thinking it might be due to particular spiritual hindrances. He considered various possibilities in turn, reflecting on a number of common attachments and mental weaknesses, wondering if it may be due to any of them that he was suffering from this terror. However, he came to realise that none of these was the cause of his reaction. He had already achieved great spiritual insights and yet he was still afflicted by fear. So it was that he decided to tackle the fear more directly:

The thought occurred to me: 'What if — on recognized, designated nights such as the eighth, fourteenth & fifteenth of the lunar fortnight — I were to stay in the sort of places that are awe-inspiring and make your hair stand on end, such as park-shrines, forest-shrines, & tree-shrines? Perhaps I would get to see that fear & terror.' So at a later time — on recognized, designated nights such as the eighth, fourteenth, & fifteenth of the lunar fortnight —

I stayed in the sort of places that are awe-inspiring and make your hair stand on end, such as park-shrines, forest-shrines & tree-shrines. And while I was staying there a wild animal would come, or a bird would make a twig fall, or wind would rustle the fallen leaves. The thought would occur to me: 'is this that fear & terror coming?' Then the thought occurred to me: 'Why do I just keep waiting for fear? What if I were to subdue fear & terror in whatever state they come?' So when fear & terror came while I was walking back & forth, I would not stand or sit or lie down. I would keep walking back & forth until I had subdued that fear & terror. When fear & terror came while I was standing, I would not walk or sit or lie down. I would keep standing until I had subdued that fear & terror. When fear & terror came while I was sitting, I would not lie down or stand up or walk. I would keep sitting until I had subdued that fear & terror. When fear & terror came while I was lying down, I would not sit up or stand or walk. I would keep lying down until I had subdued that fear & terror.[32]

This description is remarkably similar to the sort of experimentation which we might include in a modern therapeutic programme. Gotama, the man destined to become the Buddha,[33] deliberately confronts his fears by going to the places in the forest which are most frightening, namely the forest shrines, on 'designated nights', the times when spirits are believed to be there. Having recognised that, despite his spiritual journey, he is still handicapped by paralysing fear, he deliberately sets out to experiment with the situation, to identify its real nature and its causes, and to find ways of transforming and overcoming it.

At first he simply watches his mental process. He notices the way that noises in the darkness give rise to the fear and he observes the way that his mind reacts to them. This practice is something which many mindfulness practitioners would recognise. He is observing the causation of anxiety, the arising of feeling and its manifestation in a bodily response. He anticipates feeling anxiety arise as he listens for scary noises in the night. He is curious and investigative in his attitude, keen to face the impulses that come up in him and not avoid them by running away or distracting himself.

Having begun to do this, however, he then questions the nature of the fear itself, setting out to master it by deliberately facing it. It is like a process of desensitisation. Whenever the fear arises, he observes it. He does not allow himself to be deflected from experiencing it, but, rather, persists in whatever he is doing at the time when it arises until he has conquered it. If he is standing, he continues to stand; if he sits, he continues to sit. He does not allow himself to be distracted from it.

When we take ourselves into the wild, we may be confronted by primitive reactions. Our bodies are conditioned by instinctive response patterns which protect us from potential dangers. It seems that humans and animals are genetically programmed to be fearful of certain things like snakes or large animals which are likely to be predators. In the modern world we rarely feel these impulses because we do not live in circumstances where the triggers for them occur, though we can still experience these basic feelings of danger lurking in our dreams and in our unconscious. When we go out into nature, however, we may encounter raw surges of fear and dread which seem to wash over us regardless of our rational assessment of the situation we are in.

As the sutta describes, when we are frightened in this primitive way, we react viscerally. For example, the text describes the way that in scary places one's hair stands on end. In other words, we have the same response as an animal such as a dog or cat. When animals are frightened their hair stands up and their coats fluff out, so that they look larger than they really are. This is a defensive strategy, making them appear more threatening to whatever creature is approaching them.

Night can be a time when primitive fears surface. In the darkness, sounds are magnified and the eyes can be deceived by things that appear out of the half-light. Our minds are confused by sleepiness or disorientated by unusual wakefulness. So it is often at night that we experience raw fear.

I wake in the night in my tent. I am not sure what has woken me, but as I lie awake, I am suddenly caught by a flash of light. I wait, expecting thunder, but the noise never comes. There is nothing, just the darkness. I listen, my ears straining, but it is silent. I unzip the doorway, but the night is still and clear, the stars exceptionally bright. There is no cloud and no sign of an impending storm.

The thought goes through my head, "Did I imagine that flash?"

Suddenly I feel a surge of fear. Although I initially thought that I knew what the flash was, now uncertainty floods through me. I grope for an explanation, and find one that seems to amplify my anxiety. Maybe my eyes are playing tricks on me, or maybe, worse, they are not working properly.

I have an eye condition for which I normally use drops. The last few weeks, staying in the tent, I have forgotten to use them on quite a few occasions. I know I have been careless and now I have a wave of anxiety that I have caused some long-term damage by my neglect. The thought is only momentary, but it gives substance to the rising panic which I am feeling. There is a kind of logic to it, but the feeling is more deep-rooted, embedded in some more fundamental terror of the unexplained.

It is not long before rationality kicks in and tells me I am creating worries out of nothing, urging me to look again at what might have caused the flash, but in that moment I am facing raw fear. I look up again at the sky, shocked by my vulnerability. How quickly the mind can turn the unexplained into terrors.

Another flash from the southern horizon tells me that a storm is raging somewhere down in the Auvergne. On such a clear night, the lightning flashes can be seen at huge distances. Light carries more than sound and we are far out of range for hearing the thunder.

As soon as the cause of the flashing is clear, my mind changes. My anxiety disappears completely and I am suddenly interested in watching the storm, curious to see whether it might be coming our way and excited by the prospect of this possibility. My mind is now in control, directing its attention with confidence. Fear and anxiety are fickle phenomena, dependent on the imagination as much as on reality. They arise out of the gaps in our certainty, but our tendency is always to subdue them by shaping our perceptions into things which are already known and familiar.

A few nights later, I encounter this sort of primitive anxiety again. This time I am sleeping out under the stars beside the bonfire. My sleeping bag is on top of an old foam mattress with several extra old sleeping bags on top for warmth. It is very snug and comfortable and I sleep soundly, despite the falling dew, which coats my bedding with a thin film of water droplets.

It must be around four o'clock when I wake to hear a loud barking noise close by. An animal is making its way towards me through the darkness. The first sound could be a dog bark, but it is too close to me to be one of the dogs from the neighbouring farm. I wonder if it might be a fox, for we have found their droppings on the path. The next sound, however, is a strange series of grunts, like a large animal shaking its head from side to side and complaining. It is very close.

Although I know that there are no dangerous animals in France, the sound of a large animal close by in the night evokes a strong visceral reaction in me. My mind is not worried, but my body responds as it might at the sound of a lion or bear on the prowl. I feel the clenching of my stomach as the eerie grunting noise passes by, probably along the nearby track.

I do not know what the sound is. Others have reported

hearing it too. Maybe it is a stag, possibly a wild boar, for both come on to our land from time to time. In the daytime it would be exciting to see it, but now, in the middle of the night, the edge between excitement and fear is small. I lie, hardly breathing, my ears straining for more sounds for quite a while, but none come. The night is quiet now. Eventually I drift back to sleep.

In the Sutta on Fear and Dread, the Buddha describes the way that he faced out this sort of primitive, existential fear. His experience in meditative practice strengthened his ability to stand firm amid feelings of dread which came up in him in these frightening situations. Having done this, through conquering his fear, the Buddha achieved the complete insight, calmness and presence which had been evading him in his previous spiritual searching. *Unflagging persistence was aroused in me, and unmuddled mindfulness established. My body was calm & unaroused, my mind concentrated & single.* Encountering raw fear led him to break through the ordinary unenlightened mind-state and see things with a new clarity. His perspective was no longer distorted because he was able to unhook himself from the mental cycles which he came to see were associated with maintaining an illusion of security and control in the face of such fears through building the self-world.

The processes of delusion are basically concerned with protecting ourselves from our existential fears, so that when he had conquered that primitive fear, they were no longer needed. The self-building processes fell away and the Buddha now saw 'day' as 'day' and 'night' as 'night'. There was no filtering of experience. Mara, the deadness which comes from fear, was defeated.

The sutta continues with a description of the Buddha's enlightenment experience. This unfolding of insights was the spiritual consequence of the Buddha's determination to face the full force of those primitive feelings without flinching or escaping. Facing the fear and dread led to his ultimate break-through.

The Buddha's enlightenment was the culmination of his spiritual journey. The description in the sutta is somewhat formulaic, an account which is repeated in many suttas in rather similar form, but its presence in this particular text links it to the prior experience of overcoming fear and dread. The Buddha experienced a series of visionary experiences through three watches of the night which resulted in his complete enlightenment. From these flowed a number of insights, some of which later became formulated as the teachings on the Four Noble Truths and Dependent Origination.

This link between the process of facing our most primitive fears and that of achieving enlightenment is very significant in our understanding of Buddhist Psychology. It confirms the central role that affliction, *dukkha*, plays in developing spiritual maturity. Getting beyond our fears and consequent tendency to engage in compulsive avoidance activity is the driving force for spiritual growth. According to the Sutta on Fear and Dread, it was by conquering his impulses to escape that the Buddha broke through the last vestiges of attachment and thus achieved complete spiritual awakening. In other words, to fully experience *dukkha* rather than escaping from it through the distractions of the senses, of self-building and creating identity, or of seeking oblivion and self-destruction, the three levels of clinging, is to become alive to the world in a new way. This understanding became enshrined in the description of samudaya in the key Buddhist teaching, the *Four Noble Truths*.

In the Sutta on Fear and Dread, the Buddha, having pursued a path in which he had eliminated every other barrier to enlightenment and removed the hindrances and overcome delusion, still experienced fear. He had achieved everything he could through his own efforts and yet was still held by the grip of those primitive animal responses which arose in him on that instinctive level. It was in facing out this most basic fear that he finally reached the ultimate spiritual state. The truth he realised was that he did not need to fear the world. He did not have to dread others. He could allow them to speak to him. He could see them for what they really are.

Having completely overcome his fear, for the Buddha, the forests turned from frightening places into places of spiritual enrichment. With the insight which came from this experience he became the great teacher who still inspires many followers today. Dwelling in the forest became both a resource supporting him, and, through his example, a place where many lived and practised. Transforming his fear he discovered the ultimate aliveness in himself, and brought spiritual truth to free others of future generations. He expresses this at the close of the sutta. *It's through seeing two compelling reasons that I resort to isolated forest & wilderness dwellings: seeing a pleasant abiding for myself in the present, and feeling sympathy for future generations.*[34]

Whilst our own experiences of the fear and anxiety which arise in wild spaces are unlikely to bring us to the point of complete enlightenment, they do often leave us feeling more alive and more open to the world. Facing difficulties and not running away from those things which evoke terror helps us to develop spiritual and psychological maturity. Our lives are limited by our anxieties and our attempts to protect ourselves and cling to semblances of permanence. Often our existential fears are buried beneath layers of evasion which are never challenged. Working with nature can take us into the dark places which touch these very deep primitive passions[35] and thus can potentially free us from some of our layers of pretence and deadness[36] if we can have the courage to stand firm.

Chapter Fourteen

The Space Element

Some years ago I had a two-day retreat in the secret field. The field is so called because it is in the middle of our land, surrounded completely by other fields and woodland. A relatively small area, the field is contained by large oak trees which grow along the boundaries and predominate in the woods that adjoin it. There is a thick cordon of blackthorn around the edge of the field on three sides, which has overgrown into a thicket, making access from those directions impossible. The only way to reach the field is through the wood which borders it, running between it and the electricity line. It is therefore completely enclosed in the heart of the property.

The soil of the field is poor and shallow and supports only a fine, light grass, unlike the other fields which have coarse meadow grass. There are outcrops of stone in places, and areas of wild flowers which look like rock gardens.

For my retreat I took with me a large groundsheet, a sleeping bag, several bottles of water, a few basic personal items, six apples and a pot of yoghurt. I also took with me *The First Buddhist Women*[37] by Susan Murcott, a translation of the Therigata, the poems and stories of the ordained women who followed the Buddha. These were a group of strong women whose stories are fascinating and often adventurous, so I thought they would make good companions on my retreat.

I had no watch for my retreat so I could only use the sun to tell the time. Through the days I sat and walked and read within my field, venturing only as far as the path into the woods and back again. At night I tied the plastic groundsheet to an overhanging branch of one of the oak trees with a piece of string in order to make a shelter. I tied the string halfway along one side of the plastic so that the corners of it flapped down, creating a triangular apex. The sheet was long enough to curl underneath my sleeping bag. Thus I had a rudimentary tent, which offered some shelter against the elements, whilst still being open to the wind.

I had no prescribed pattern for my retreat. I followed my intuition, spending some time sitting in meditation, some chanting, some reading the poetry and stories and some walking. I watched the days turn through their cycle, the sun rising over the trees behind my sleeping area and gradually coming into view, traversing the sky and dipping low over the hedge on the far side of the field. I paced my day accordingly, practising at times when it felt right to do so, and eating my apples and yogurt, my only food, following my body's needs and the movement of the sun. I slept when it got dark and woke when the sun rose. I listened to the creatures around me and shared their rhythms.

As I sat quietly, the animals started to lose their timidity. Birds and squirrels went about their business in the branches above me and in the undergrowth deeper into the wood. A pigmy shrew turned out to have its home right next to my camping site. I got to know this tiny creature as it scurried about in the fallen oak leaves, rooting around for grubs and other food, unperturbed by my presence. Pigmy shrews, one of the tiniest of mammals in Europe, have pointed snouts for foraging and sniffing out their prey, sharp beady eyes, and rounded bodies. They look cute, but they can be ferocious. Just after my retreat, David also used the bivvy for a retreat, and, while there, he witnessed the same shrew locked in a terrible battle of primeval proportions with a slow worm.

On the second night as I slept in my improvised shelter, I woke to hear a much larger creature scuffling about in the undergrowth nearby. I never found out what it was. Half asleep,

I lay motionless for a few minutes, my breathing held tight against a rush of unformed feelings of anxiety, my heart pounding, and ears straining to make out the source of the sound. In my sleepiness I imagined that a wild boar was close at hand, about to come thundering into my clearing and trample all over me.

Of course, if it had appeared, a boar would have been more frightened than I was. Wild boars are shy creatures, and avoid contact with humans. It would have run away at the first scent of me. In all probability what I heard was actually a hedgehog, shuffling on its nightly meanderings. In the night, however, as we have already reflected, noises are magnified and the dream-soaked mind leaps into creating the craziest fantasies. As I gradually came to full wakefulness, I worked all this out and was able to laugh at myself, but the image which my imagination conjured up of a big hairy, tusked boar bearing down on me through the bushes and brambles, nostrils flayed and a menacing look in its eye is still clear in my memories of the retreat.

In an intensive period of retreat we face our demons. The mind runs through all its usual patterns of resistance. There are periods of boredom and frustration or fear and anger, cravings and grandiose plans. Whatever our habitual thoughts and feelings are, they surface on the empty face of unstructured time.

It is striking how persistent this pattern is, even in very different kinds of retreat. People are often surprised, for example, to discover that an intensive chanting retreat throws up just the same mental processes as a silent sitting retreat does. An unstructured solitary retreat invites the same mental games as a timetabled one.

Of course, there are also particulars. On a solitary retreat we have to face more starkly the fact that we are authors of these processes. When we are in a group, we can blame others for our difficulties, but when we are on retreat alone, there is no one else on whom we can pin the discomforts or frustrations. We cannot blame others for our irritations or seek in them relief for our fears and anxieties. When we are on our own, it is evident that these demons are entirely of our own creation.

Also, though, a solitary retreat faces us with the basic truth of our isolation. Although, as human beings, we are in one sense connected to others, dependent on them, and unable to live without their support and cooperation, in another sense we are each on our own. No matter how close we are to loved ones, family and friends, all our relationships are subject to impermanence, as we are ourselves. People die or quarrel with one another, move away to far-off places, change their interests, or fall in love with other people. Even those to whom we are closest remain a mystery to us and sometimes behave in ways which we do not recognise. Ultimately we face death on our own, as far as we know without human companions to travel with us beyond the portal of this life. It is only by looking beyond the human realm that we can feel enduring support in such circumstances.

A solitary retreat in nature immerses us in life. We see our minds' unfolding soap opera of thoughts and dreams, but this becomes a thin veneer against the intensity of living processes with which we are in touch, if we allow ourselves to be alone and still.

Whilst on my retreat, I was accompanied by the early nuns. I read their stories of spiritual breakthrough. Some stories expressed grief for loved ones whom they had lost, for many of the women came to the religious life through personal tragedy. Others expressed regrets for events of the past. Some voiced ironic humour in the face of passing years, as time took its toll on health and beauty. I read of the feelings of sisterhood between the members of the group, and the support and love they shared. In particular I read about how their lives were grounded in the natural processes of earth and nature, birth and death and loving. They found their inspiration in the practices which brought them back to the basic elements of life: earth, air, fire, water, space. They appreciated ordinary things. Down the centuries I felt connection with this experience. The processes of women's lives, transformed by their shared faith and practices, became the source of their enlightenment.

During my retreat I developed a particular practice of doing walking meditation with my eyes closed. I would stand on the path which goes through the woods, looking ahead of me in the direction in which I was going to walk. I would then shut my eyes and focus my attention on the sensation of standing, being aware of my feet on the ground and the solidity of the soil beneath me. I would feel my presence in the wood, a sense of being among the trees and undergrowth. I would smell the leaf mould and mossy dampness of the dark corners where sun didn't reach. I would sense the light filtering down through the branches overhead, feeling its warmth on my skin, recalling the dappling of shadows which it cast on the path in front of me.

Then, having grounded myself in this way, I would walk forwards slowly for twenty steps, keeping my eyes closed and placing my feet by feel and by memory of the way. Walking with the eyes closed intensifies the experience of contact with the ground. Each stone, each twig, each irregularity of the earth is felt through the sole of the foot, and gently accommodated as the weight is placed upon it. In the darkness, one takes more care. One also discovers a new kind of trust. One trusts that the space ahead will be clear. One trusts the senses of touch and hearing, and using them in new, more intensive ways.

Feeling my way forward, sensing the presence of tree trunks or brambles but not knowing exactly where they were, I experienced a new intensity of encounter with the forest. On the twentieth step I stopped. Standing still, I opened my eyes. Before me there would be something. It might be a plant, a tree, a vista, a scene. Something would be there in front of me to catch my eye. I repeated this sequence a number of times. Twenty steps with eyes closed, then opening my eyes to look at whatever was in front of me. Each time I stopped and opened my eyes, I would invite the forest to present me with an object.

Life presents us with gifts of beauty and fascination all the time and we walk right past them with hardly a second glance. Looking at whatever appeared to me in the moment when I opened my eyes, I practised stopping and honouring the experience, giving the object my full attention for five long breaths, before closing my eyes once more and taking the next twenty steps forward.

This practice left me with a series of strong images of places and objects in the woods. The meditation created a magnifying glass whereby the apparently ordinary became special and even spectacular. Each time I opened my eyes, I felt as if I was seeing the world for the first time. Each sight was bright and clear and beautiful in its particularity.

One occasion especially still stays vivid in my mind. This time on opening my eyes I found that I was facing the trunk of a tree. It was not an especially big tree, for, though fully grown, its girth was moderate. For me, though, in that moment, it was perfect. The bark was fairly smooth and grey, flecked with darker patterning. The sunlight caught it, sharpening the contrasts. Although it was in one way just another tree, I stood, transfixed by the intensity of colour and texture.

Tree bark is pretty ordinary stuff. There is a lot of it about. But it is also extraordinary; a huge variety of colours, textures, markings. Seeing that tree bark in this clear, unguarded way touched me in a way that has remained vivid, a promise of a possibility for a different way of being alive.

When we break through the veils of ordinary mind and look again, we see differently. We witness a world no longer influenced by the contamination of interpretation and grasping habits. This way of seeing is beyond our ordinary capacities of seeing, and, indeed, even our brightest glimpses of the world, like my experience of the tree bark, are still clouded with many degrees of filtering. But when we come close to such experience, we see the radiance of life. We look into the space which is beyond our mental games and see spiritual reality. This is what in Buddhism is sometimes referred to as emptiness or space, the absence of self-interest in our view; the clear bright mirror mind which sees what is.

Nature wakes us up by her abundance. The clamour of life in a wild place breaks in on our self-preoccupation and bids us pay attention, not to our mind's eternal ramblings, but to the glorious unfolding of bigger processes of which we are only a tiny part. Structures create space. The structures of a retreat, or of spiritual practices within such a retreat, create the space for such an opening, however brief, but it is the natural world itself which finds those gaps and reveals itself to us.

Even though it is now perhaps eight years since that retreat, the experiences of it remain current in my life, moments of inspiration that still reverberate. This is the gift of the solitary retreat in nature. It changes us if we allow it to.

There have always been hermits and solitary practitioners in Buddhism. Although shared practice is immensely important and is one of the foundations of the tradition, periods of separation are also part of the spiritual tradition.

The mountain or the cave, the forest hut or the open road, are places of intense practice. Serious practitioners often adopt such places, if only for limited periods. Sometimes such retreats are focused on an inner journey, the practitioner delving unhindered by worldly distraction into the deepest recesses of mind. The mould grows on the soup pot whilst the master meditates. Birds reportedly nested in Bodhidharma's hair whilst he spent his eight years facing the wall in fifth century China. Others, though, find spiritual truth in nature. The poetry of Saigyo and the other Japanese poet monks bears witness to solitary engagement with living creatures, plants and the elemental forces of the weather and seasons.

A solitary retreat creates space in our lives. It opens up a possibility for new things to emerge and for us to let go of some of our habituated thoughts and behaviours so that we can allow those things which are greater than we are, which are beyond our usual experience, to speak to us. When we create such a space in our lives, we are working with the last of the five elements in the Buddhist system, the element of space.

The space element can be understood in two ways. On the one hand it is seen as the gaps in the world. We have already seen how structures create spaces and how the objects which furnish our worlds have gaps between them; how the boundaries which define a space influence the quality of the space which they enclose. This is one way of thinking about the space element.

The space element is also an area of potential, a space into which things can emerge, where there is no obstruction. It is an invitation to things to be. Giving something space, we invite its presence. Giving people space, we respect their capacity to speak and act. Giving life space we invite the world to speak to us.

Thus space can be an absence and a fullness. Of course, these two meanings converge. When we create spaces between structures, say in planting a hedge around an area which we call a field, we also invite that field to grow into something. The hedge creates a potential for a field to emerge, but the field itself changes and flourishes within that space. If we do nothing to create other things within it, such as by planting crops, nature will fill the field in its own way, with dandelions or blackthorn or ants nests or brambles.

This same relationship between creating a structure and leaving a space happens at a psychological and spiritual level, as can be seen in the solitary retreat. We go away into an isolated place and we set up certain conditions. We change the normal structures of our day. We create a space in which something happens that we cannot predict or control. Something then arrives. Through taking retreat time, unpredictable processes unfold. Insights arise. Beauty manifests.

Whether the structure is physical or psychological, it holds open the space. Making a fence, we protect the area of ground from wandering animals or wind or invading scrub or other humans. Creating a retreat space, we set a period of time apart and keep out intrusions such as the telephone or news media or conversations with friends. Holding back those things which would intrude and take over the space, something new, something other, can be present.

As with the other elements, the space element can be explored as it occurs in the world around us, as it occurs in the physical structure of the body, and as a metaphor for the psychological processes which unfold in the mind.

When we look at the spaces in the body, we find that the body contains a series of cavities; the nasal cavity, the chest, the abdominal cavity, the cranial cavity, the womb and so on. All provide spaces, protected by bones and muscles within which various processes and organs operate. Some of these cavities have openings to the external space of the world. The nasal cavity opens through the nostrils. The intestinal cavity opens through the mouth and anus. Through these openings passes material which is not itself part of the body, such as air or food or faeces. These parts of the body are open to the external world because the opening is necessary to its function. Other cavities are enclosed and separated from the outside world by screens of tissue. For example although the interior of the gut is necessarily open to the external world at both ends, the abdominal cavity must remain separated from it or else peritonitis will set it. Its enclosure protects it from bacteria which would multiply and infect it causing serious illness or death.

Some cavities have soft casings which can yield and stretch, like the muscle wall of the abdomen, but others are hard and rigid, formed by bones such as the skull and the ribs. The cranium contains the brain and the chest cavity the heart and lungs. Whether the cavity protects a bodily organ, or allows the movement of non-body products, however, the structure and its contents remain separate and do not contaminate one another. The space allows movement and keeps the content and container distinct. Separation is thus just as important a quality of spaces as the space itself.

We can also think of the space aspect of the body in another way. The body itself takes up space. It occupies space in the universe which might otherwise be occupied by other things. In this respect it has equivalence with all matter. If this piece of universe is not occupied by my arm, it will be occupied by air, or a piece of furniture, or someone else's arm. We just take up space like everything else takes up space.

In reflecting on the way we take up space, we can reflect on our merits from the perspective of the universe. Our presence is beneficial to some things and problematic to others. We tend to think of ourselves as special, and as relating to the world as if from some unique vantage point. When we think of the way our body is simply an area of space, however, our mental map is realigned. We are just another configuration of matter, occupying space within a field of matter. We are just contents in the space of the universe. We occupy the spaces which are created by its structures.

There is a concept in Buddhism which is called sunyata. Sunyata is often translated as emptiness. In this, it can be understood to mean space. This meaning of emptiness or space is, however, quite particular.

Sunyata means the absence of self. It is a description of what is experienced when we take away the self-preoccupation which normally contaminates our view of everything. Since removing our self-centred viewpoint from perception is something which we are unlikely to fully accomplish, the concept is an ideal, a theoretical possibility, rather than a state we are likely to attain in ordinary life.

When we meditate or create a retreat space we try to reduce the mind's tendency to rush in and contaminate all that it sees with self-interested thoughts and habits so that we can see things more clearly as they really are. In as much as we are successful, the experience of a retreat often becomes one of seeing things more intensively. Once the mind has got through its resistances and stopped clinging so tightly to the old patterns of thinking, it starts to see things more freshly. This can be an irritating and educative process to go through, as well as a liberating one, because we are used to our old patterns of thinking and seeing, and retreats are not always comfortable occasions. The end of a retreat, however, is often characterised by a feeling of heightened perception. The world seems beautiful and bright, shining and radiant. In the structured regime of the retreat, we have let go of some of the dulling effects of habit, and allowed space for the world to shine through in all its brightness.

Emptiness in Buddhism is not therefore about total absence. It is not a dead space. It could equally be called presence. It is about allowing space for the full presence of the real world to emerge by holding back the intruding effects of habit and self. Just like the fence which keeps straying animals at bay, so too the retreat structures hold back the chatter of thoughts and everyday activity, giving space for the world to shine in unhindered.

In a recent interview,[38] Dale Griffin, the former drummer from the group Mott the Hoople, talked about his experience of developing Alzheimer's disease. It was a moving interview.

Despite having evidently lost some cognitive faculties, Dale struggled to describe his frustration with the effects which the disease was already having on him. He talked of his uncertainty about the future, facing further losses of mental acuity. Often searching for language to express his thoughts, for words themselves did not come easily to him any longer, he described what it was like suffering from the disease.

"What it is," he said, ironically, "is this huge empty space – that's [its] gift for me."

The space which Alzheimer's gave to Dale was not one he appreciated. He feared its increasing hold on his mind, the losses which it already involved, and the further spaces which it would create in his life.

Sunyata is not a space of this kind. It is not a loss of mental faculty or a process of shutting down and closing off from experience. Rather it is about opening up. In the state of sunyata, the voices and assumptions which our minds create, which limit our experience, stop. We pull back the curtain of self-preoccupation which cuts us off from the world and, in as much as we are able, we walk out into the spaciousness of experience. We end our habitual chattering and allow the other to speak to us.

Chapter Fifteen

Gazing at Stars

The campfire is dying down. We have sung folk songs and chanted harmonies from Taizé as well as Buddhist chants. We have made cocoa and toasted bread on the embers, held out to the glowing remains of the fire on pronged twigs rescued from the woodpile. Now we are relaxing in the field. The night is crystal clear, and as the last glow of the orange sunset starts to fade to a pale liquid turquoise, the first stars are coming out. Venus is bright in the south-west. This planet follows close to the sun and is moving downward toward the horizon. Overhead, the summer triangle is already visible.

We have planned to have a late group under the stars on another evening, but, as weather is always unpredictable, Sundari and I wonder if we should change our plans and watch the stars tonight. Discussion follows. If we are going to stay out, we should all agree on it so that the whole group shares the experience. There is general enthusiasm for the idea.

So it is that we return to the house to hastily gather ground sheets and old sleeping bags. Once the sun goes down, on a clear night, it can get very cold even in early August. We do not want the fire to be too bright or it will mask the stars.

We create our group space near to the stone fire place in the middle of the field on an area of flat ground. Spreading out the tarpaulins, we cover them with a few of the sleeping bags to create a place big enough for us all to lie comfortably. We then form a circle, lying on our backs, with heads into the centre of the group so that we can talk and hear one another easily, tucking ourselves around with more of the sleeping bags so that we will keep warm as we watch the sky.

It is quiet. The sunset has faded to a faint pale glow on the western horizon and many more stars have appeared, but it is still not fully dark. As we lie, people talk of memories of childhood. One person recalls going out with her father to watch the stars, some others remember names of constellations. We identify the plough, Cassiopeia, Cygnus and the Pole Star. We speculate about other star groups. There are memories of camping holidays and sleepovers with friends. We chat, recalling our childhoods, and sometimes feeling as if we are still children, enjoying a rare late night treat.

As the sky gradually becomes darker, the stars become brighter. The moon is waning so has not yet risen. Fainter stars begin to fill the gaps between the main constellations. The Milky Way sweeps its arc across the bowl of the heavens, its outline, with its dark patches and projecting fingers of light, becoming clear against the darkness. Satellites and aircraft traverse the sky, the latter winking red or white, the former moving smoothly and slowly as they circle the earth; points of light, like the stars which form the backdrop against which they move, distinguishable only by their steady, unwavering progress.

Occasionally across this silent vista, a meteor streams its course. We are nearing the peak of the Perseids, and we anticipate that tonight will be a good opportunity to watch shooting stars. There are many of them. Some are faint, glimpsed from the corner of the eye and gone almost before they are registered, but some are bright, compelling, leaving trails of light across the sky for seconds as they plummet through the outer layers of atmosphere.

"Let's be silent for a minute," I suggest.

The chatter stops. Everyone is quiet, watching. We breathe into the silence. The air is sharp as cold water. Only the distant sound of a dog in the stillness seems to intensify the absence of noise. Precise as the points of light in the black sky, it penetrates the night.

I invite the group to be aware of the vastness of space as we look up into the dome of the sky. These tiny points of light, each a sun, some many times bigger than our own solar system, some in fact galaxies, are so far away we cannot conceive their distance. Just as an ant could not envisage a human city, so too our tininess and vulnerability makes us incapable of appreciating the scale of what we see. As we look out, we not only stare into expanses so great that we can hardly envisage them, but also we gaze back in time to stars and systems that will have already changed by now, whose light began its journey many centuries ago. Some of what we see is light emitted before human life even began. The nearest star is four light years away and most are far more distant.

Looking up, we are one with our ancestors, who saw the heavens and in them read guidance for their lives. United by this ancient companion, the clear night sky, we can experience something of that wonder and respect for the stars which humans have felt down the centuries.

In our modern lives we can go for days or weeks or months without looking up into the heavens and we can start to feel ourselves omnipotent. It is only by looking outward to the great dance of space, in which the creation and destruction of solar systems is just part of a bigger, more beautiful story, that we learn humility. With these reflections, we lie, silently looking up.

Then slowly people start to share, now more quietly, reflecting on the sense of awe they feel in the face of these thoughts. Is there, in all that great sea of space, other life? And if there were, could we communicate with it? Why do we assume it to be of our ilk, intelligent, capable of language, of similar size and substance? We have spent days watching and encountering the life around us, yet even with our common evolutionary threads, our shared DNA, we cannot communicate with our fellow creatures on this planet. And what can we understand of spiritual truths? What meaning, if any, could encompass this immeasurable void, filled with so many unknown worlds? How could we as humans, inhabiting one small speck of dust within this universe, understand and name its meaning?

Shooting stars streak across the sky, breaking in on our ruminations. Some are bright enough to evoke gasps of excitement. Their unpredictability keeps us always thirsting for the next sighting. It is impossible to watch the whole sky, so we are always missing ones that others see. Each cry of excitement is echoed by others exclaiming, "What? Where was it? I missed that one."

The experience is intoxicating. Each meteor leaves us wanting more and, even though it is getting late, we are reluctant to go to bed. It is too easy to think, "I will just wait for one more good one, then I'll go."

The night goes on and the stars creep round the heavens. The Milky Way changes its angle.

Eventually, though, people are getting too tired to stay up any longer. We may sleep out in the open later in the week, but tonight we are not prepared and do not have enough bedding. Heavy eyed, reluctantly, one by one, we get up from the warm nest of blankets that we have created and depart into the chill of the night.

It is very dark and, with the darkness and the clear sky, dew is already forming. The covers are getting damp and the grass is wet under foot. The air feels sharp as we breathe.

Carefully we make our way back across the field to the house and to the lights of the kitchen. The path is uneven and hard to follow in the dark, so we fumble our way, feet searching out the well-trodden route, and occasionally missing it. We find ourselves wading unintentionally into the field grass through which it is cut, having to backtrack on to the firmer ground of the path. It is good to rely on our sense of touch, our feet's capacity to find their way even when the visibility is so poor.

In the overgrown edges of the path we see glow-worms, tiny

pinpricks of silver-blue light, bright as the stars above our heads. It is amazing to see how such creatures produce light chemically, signalling to their mates through the darkness.

Later I walk across to my tent on the far side of the orchard. Some of the group are sleeping in the buildings, others are in tents scattered across the field around the house. The stars are still bright and I am tempted to look for just one more shooting star, but, knowing I have a group to lead in the morning I reluctantly climb inside and close the zip.

When I was a child Orion lived at the front of our house. The Plough was in the back garden. The stars were part of my early childhood, for the house in which these constellations dwelt was the one which I lived in until I was seven. In retrospect I realise that these familiar figures were in the winter sky, for summer evenings were times when I would 'go to bed by day' to quote Robert Louis Stevenson.[39] Summer evenings I listened to the swish, swish of the hand pushed lawnmower as my father cut the lawn. Winter nights he took me out to look at the stars. That was when we lived in the country, a small village called Rough Common on the edge of Canterbury.

When I was seven we moved to London where the orange sodium street lights blocked out the stars. For a long time there I thought the sky was red because something close by was on fire. It frightened me.

I loved looking up at the constellations. I didn't know many, but I learned to recognise the Seven Sisters and Sirius the Dog Star. I learned to spot Aldebaran, the red eye of Taurus the bull, in the great V of the beast's horned face. I knew the story of how Orion and his dogs chased it across the sky. When it was clear you could see Orion's Belt and even his shield, a big oval of stars in front of the figure.

But then I started to learn more about stars. When I moved to London I joined the local children's library and borrowed books which told me about white dwarfs and red giants. These terrified me. A red giant was so big that it would engulf the inner planets of our solar system they told me. One day our sun would become a red giant just like Aldebaran, with a gravity field so big that by then the earth would have been swallowed up by it.

It was no good my parents reassuring me that when that happened, they, I and everyone we knew would be long since dead. I still lay awake at night, horrified at the prospect of everything I loved disappearing into a great conflagration.

Perhaps children just have better imaginations than adults. I rarely worry about red giants these days. But I guess that as adults we have more immediate concerns. Perhaps, as the kindly gentleman at the London Planetarium reassured us when we visited with the school, by the time the sun becomes a red giant, we will all have jumped into our spaceships and gone off to find somewhere else to live. That was the sixties, and people were optimistic in those days. Today we face different concerns about the destruction of our planet, or at least of its eco-systems, which are far closer at hand, but no one feels reassured that anyone is going to make the getaway car.

But still, despite my fears, I continued to look for the stars. Still when the Plough is overhead or Orion rises before dawn, I look up into the heavens and see friends. Our own planet wheels on its journey, but the stars hardly change with the centuries.

Recently I was sitting in a small planetarium with my own now adult children. We were in Newcastle and had popped into the local museum, where I used to take them as children, for old times' sake. The planetarium was new, tucked into a corner on the top floor. There were not many other visitors. We took our seats on the plush sofas and waited for the room to darken.

The projector started to turn, wheeling us up through our

familiar spiral galaxy. This was not a simple recreation of the night sky, but was to be a show which described the further reaches of space and new discoveries about its nature. Out into the darkest, deepest space we went on our imaginary journey. The American commentary elaborated the process as we travelled, peppering facts with superlatives and exclamations. Spirals and dots flew across the domed screen. The simulated speed was huge. World, stars, galaxies, receded.

And then, suddenly I saw it. The utterly small dot that was supposed to be our galaxy, imaged in a huge field of other similar dots, like scattered rice grains on a tabletop. There, from a vantage point so very far off in deepest unimaginable space, everything we ever see, even the myriad stars in the great firmament, which are mostly part of our own galaxy, were so inconceivably small as to have disappeared into the tiny blur of light. Our own sun was far too small to be distinguished amongst them, and the earth had become molecular in scale.

The penny dropped. At that moment I saw just how vast the known universe is. At that moment I knew that even the known universe was only part of what may be beyond it. At that moment I saw how tiny this planet was in the great scheme of things, and how impossibly small I and my concerns were.

We can know these things at an intellectual level and can discuss them theoretically, but to actually see how, on the scale of the universe, everything that we are and love is so tiny that it becomes virtually invisible, involves a shift of mind which shakes us out of our complacency. In such a moment, the mind hovers between futility and awe, strung out by spiralling numbers.

We returned to the world, our eyes a little clearer.

The astronauts were changed by seeing the earth from space. Several found spiritual paths, but others were psychologically unsettled by their experiences. Life hangs in the balance, a blue green sphere in a great sea of blackness. I filed out of the planetarium with my children, grateful for the preciousness of human connection between us.

It is getting towards the end of summer, and the nights are getting colder. The sun sinks behind the trees earlier now, and by nine it is dark. Venus is bright on the western horizon and the stars overhead are appearing as sharp pin heads in the chilly air. Above my head the plough still rides high, its tail pointing down to Arcturus, the bright orange star in Boötes, the hunter. I remember this star from my teenage years, for it used to shine in through my bedroom window. It took me a while to identify it then, as it was so bright I thought it must be a planet. Arching across the sky, the Milky Way is visible, though partially obscured by light trails of cloud which drift across it.

The moon is in its last quarter now, rising late behind the trees of the bonfire field, but as I walk across the yard it is so bright that its light casts shadows across the gravel and throws the fennel plants, now tall and almost devoid of leaves, with large seed heads which stretch out thin spidery fingers against the sky, into a dramatic forest of vertical lines.

Although I watch for a while there are no shooting stars to be seen. We are well past the Perseids now, and their frequency has returned to normal, still a few per hour, but I am not lucky as I stand at my tent door. Summer is nearly over, but the stars remain a constant, turning their nightly course as the year makes its progress. The immensity of space is still a mystery to me, a receding page of numbers which becomes more baffling as I think about it, and even our own galaxy seems impossibly big to imagine. For all my knowledge of geography and astronomy, I can still feel connection with the times when the world was flat and the stars circled the dome of the sky as if on tiny invisible rail tracks. This feeling gives me a sense of order. All is right with the world once more.

Chapter Sixteen

Ritual and Shamanic Journey

We start in the meditation hall, gathered around the shrine in a semicircle, standing. After chanting for a few minutes, Kaspa takes a candle and lights it from the tea lights on the main shrine. He has made a lantern from a tall jam jar with a string-handle twisted around its neck and a collar of marjoram flowers. This is the last evening of the group and we have decided to have a ritual around the fireplace to mark it.

Several of us have spent time preparing the site. We have done practical things, such as collecting wood and building a fire in the stone fire circle ready for the ceremonial beginning of the evening. We have also decorated the route to the meeting space with flowers hung on cotton thread from lines strung between the trees on either side of the track, and we have created an entrance to the cut area of grass that surrounds the fire, an archway made out of branches entwined with bindweed and wild clematis from the hedge.

Having finished the chant and spoken some opening words, we process from the hall into the yard. Kaspa leads the way. He carries the lantern high and walks slowly and silently. We all follow in a line, also in silence, walking gently, our feet touching the earth with care and awareness. There is an atmosphere of concentration and reverence. In part this focus has been created by the initial ceremony in the shrine area, but it has also been enabled by the exercises of the previous five days.

We walk through the field in which the house stands and on into the adjacent one where the fire place is. The bonfire field is a large, flat field, dotted with hawthorns and saplings of oak and field-maple, with a big expanse of sky, perfect for watching the stars. The sun is low, just sinking behind the trees on the far side of the field, tingeing the sky with a pale golden glow which will gradually fade through orange, pink and deep red as the sun sets.

When we get to the fire place, we all stand once again in a circle in silence whilst Kaspa lights the fire from his candle. He kneels at one end of the stone pit, using a candle to transfer the flame to the dry hay which we have used as kindling. The flames whip through beneath the twigs as everything is very dry after the hot weather of the week. Soon the fire is fully alight and burning fiercely. We sit about it in silence.

As it happens, the needs of the group, expressed in a sharing session earlier in the day, are varied. Some want to sit up all night. Others are tired and want to sleep. Some want to undertake personal challenges. It has not been easy to arrive at a final evening ceremony which will meet everyone's preferences and we have gone through a long process of debating different possibilities.

Out of this diversity, Kaspa has proposed a ritual. We will create a sacred space, a central meeting point for all the different needs. From this central place, group members can go forth and return as they feel moved. The fire will be our focus as it has been an important part of our activities during the week. It already feels special to us, but the ritual will reinforce this feeling and consolidate its role as the spiritual centre for tonight's activities.

We have agreed to keep silence around the fire, except when someone feels moved to begin a chant. Everyone sits, watching the flames in silence. After a few minutes I start a chant. I begin 'Om Mane Padme Hum Rhi', the traditional Buddhist chant associated with Quan Shi Yin, who represents Compassion. I choose a deep, resonant tune, coming from a Tibetan tradition. As we chant, I imagine Tibetans of long ago, wrapped in their brightly coloured robes and gathered around a fire pit.

We chant for some time. The tones blend with the noises of evening, crickets and grasshoppers and an owl in the neighbouring wood. They float beneath the sounds of the evening like a soft, autumnal mist enveloping a valley among the mountains. Deep and earthy, they seem to belong to the outdoors and the spaciousness of earth and sky. When the chanting fades, there is silence, sharpened only by a dog barking in a neighbouring farm and the grasshoppers' chorus.

After a while, someone starts another chant, nembutsu this time, the call to the immeasurable. Lighter, more melodious, this chant is haunting, wistful, drifting out on the air among the insects and homecoming birds. Once again others join in. Some give voice, some listen and sit watching the fire. The sound dances heavenward in the smoke. Then, gradually, as the voices fade, again we welcome the intensity of soundlessness.

It is getting dark. The stars are appearing overhead, and the shapes of the hawthorns and bramble patches which surround the fire circle are becoming dark silhouettes against the remnants of daylight. With the fading of the sun, the collective ceremony is at an end and now we will go our different ways. A couple of people bow and leave the circle. Another, who has decided to walk all night in a solitary journey, also makes his departure to encouraging waves from the group. He will spend the hours of darkness walking along our neighbouring canal bank. Four hours in one direction and four hours back again, facing personal demons as he does so. The rest of us continue to sit, watching the fire and occasionally adding more wood. Night is with us and the collective part of the ritual is complete, but we keep the silent vigil, preserving the space for those who continue on individual paths. Some will remain to guard the fire, sleeping under the stars beside it. Others go, either to walk or to sleep. We have handed our chanting over to the night.

Journeying is a theme which emerges again and again in the

spiritual context. There are many old churches in our area of France. Quite a few are on the old pilgrim routes which fan out across France and which culminate in the great pilgrimage centre of Santiago de Compostela in Northern Spain. One branch of this network passes within a couple of miles of our centre, joining the towpath of a disused canal a mile or two north of us. From time to time we meet walkers on this route and one can find the characteristic scallop shells, the sign carried by pilgrims on the way, on several of the old churches in the vicinity.

Spending time in these old churches or walking sections of the path can give one a strong sense of connection to the spiritual legacy of European religious practice. The traces left by thousands of pilgrims down the years, both in stone and in devotional energy, replenish the spirit and support our modern contemplations. There is something about the notion of pilgrimage which satisfies a deep yearning in many of us. The life journey, and the search for resolution, be it in a spiritual epiphany, a personal emancipation, or a homecoming, are archetypal themes which resonate in the personage of the pilgrim. So in inhabiting spaces, we may also seek to travel through them towards some ultimate sacred place.

Walking in the footsteps of pilgrims is still popular. In some areas of France where the paths are better known as pilgrimage routes, one encounters many walkers making their way southwest. In particular at centres like Conques in the south of the Central Massif, and at places where the routes converge to cross the Pyrenees, one passes many young people with heavy boots, wooden staffs, and backpacks sporting scallop shells. A few years ago I was near to Conques when I met two young women, students I would guess, who were struggling along the route with a rather wayward donkey. I think the donkey was supposed to be carrying their baggage, but clearly it had gained the upper hand as the two girls were struggling under heavy packs, looking very red faced with heat and irritation, as they tried to drag the beast away from the lush grass by the roadside. The donkey seemed quite unconcerned and almost to be smiling to itself as it nonchalantly gave in to their pressure, ambling forwards a few yards before plunging its nose into the long grass on the other bank of the road. I often wondered if they ever made it to Santiago de Compostela.

Some people do these walks for personal challenge. The achievement of completing one of the great long distance footpaths of Europe must be a great source of satisfaction. But also, for many, the attraction is in the sense of walking in the footsteps of the pilgrims of previous ages, and of resonating with the history that the path represents. Within the desire to connect to the past there probably lies some intuition of the sacred purpose of the walk and its spiritual legacy, even where this is not explicit or conscious. Even the most hardened walker probably has some feeling for the spiritual meaning of the path, though it may be formulated in terms of a sense of beauty and connection with the natural elements. For some pilgrims today, however, the sense of making a religious journey is still an intentional process and the main purpose of their walk.

The idea of spiritual journey can be expressed in a real expedition, as for example in the long distance walk, but it can also take more metaphoric forms. Many people conceive of their personal process of spiritual exploration as one of travelling. With antecedents in works such as Bunyan's *Pilgrim's Progress* or, more recently, Scott Peck's *The Road Less Traveled*, the idea of the spiritual life as a journey is common in literature. So in the theme of pilgrimage, metaphor and reality come together.

Pilgrimage is often undertaken on foot. In many ways to do anything else, except perhaps prostrating one's way between holy sites, seems to be to miss the point. The classic picture of sandaled feet treading the dusty path speaks of this devotional journey. The connection between foot and earth, of course, is one which we have explored throughout this book, a step by step experience of refuge, arriving in every moment of the journey. In this way, pilgrimage has two focuses, the journey and the arrival.

As with many things in life, the journey can sometimes be more interesting than its end point. When I was sixteen I walked from Guildford to Canterbury along the old Pilgrim's Way which follows the North Downs. With a group of friends, we walked the hundred miles or so, anticipating a breathtaking arrival in Canterbury Cathedral. In fact, though the walk itself was something which became part of the folklore of our group, the long awaited arrival was rather an anticlimax. Of course the cathedral was beautiful, its fine perpendicular architecture offering a stunning spectacle among the quaint old streets of the historic Kentish town, but our arrival there was neither a spiritual nor emotional high. The place was crowded with tourists and shoppers and hardly exuded a spiritual atmosphere on the July afternoon as we wandered round, a bit bemused on our blistered feet, before heading off to find the youth hostel and our beds for the night.

"It this it?" we thought.

But in retrospect, 'it' was the walking, the journey. That journey was, in a way, a rite of passage. The first trip away from home on our own which we had organised for ourselves, it had challenged us. We had navigated our way using one-inch Ordinance Survey maps, followed overgrown footpaths, got lost, but always found our destinations in the end. We had carried our provisions on our backs, feeling for the first time the luxurious freedom of needing nothing more than we had with us. We had shopped and cooked along the way, learning to budget our pocket money and judge quantities. We had walked long distances, having sometimes overestimated our capabilities, and yet had still managed to finish each night at the pre-booked hostel.

Although we did other walks together in subsequent school holidays, none of these lived up to that first occasion when we had been pilgrims. The walk became a memory that we drew on, an icon which stood with us in our transition into adult life. It was a representation of what we were capable of, what we could be; but more, it was an experience of our connection to the earth. Walking the hills and fields of Surrey and Kent, we touched the earth, and breathed the air of the English countryside. This was the great initiation which inspired each of us to a future in which care for the planet has remained a significant concern.

Shamanic work is often associated with the natural world. It is also associated with journeying and the transitional spaces between worlds. The shaman is a person able to travel with greater freedom than is common, leaving the mundane world of ordinary human process for the realm of spirit, and therein discovering resources which can be brought back into mundane life. A messenger, a traveller, a companion or a substitute, the shaman employs trance and altered mental states to enter into those realms which are generally unseen. There he or she may alter conditions which affect others, resulting in healing, insight or the discovery of new resources.

Whilst this book is not primarily about shamanic work, the influence of shamanic thinking on environmental therapies is significant so in this chapter we will at least touch on some of the areas it addresses. These may include creating spaces for participants to dialogue with influences and forces outside their ordinary experience through imaginative and expressive work, working with different states of consciousness, and creating means for spiritual journeying.

Among these different modes of shamanic practice, one structure which often informs this kind of work is that of the vision quest. Often associated with Native American cultures, forms of vision quest in fact exist in many societies which have traditional shamanic roots. Some Buddhist practices themselves appear to have shamanic qualities and probably draw on earlier shamanic practices. In Japanese Buddhism, for example, intensive retreats were undertaken on Mount Hiei over periods of ninety days. In these events, nembutsu was chanted continuously by the devotees, who walked around inside the temple as they chanted with the aim of achieving a visionary experience of Amida Buddha.

The vision quest can be an initiation, undertaken by all members of the group, for example, at the threshold to adulthood, or it can be a practice undertaken by a solitary person as part of their individual journey or on behalf of the community as a whole. As a spiritual journey, it is often undertaken in wild spaces. The quest takes the person out of the normal structures and thought processes of society, exposing them to trials and hardships, which might come from the arduous nature of the journey itself and or from additional practices such as fasting or sleep deprivation.

It is a journey into a solitary place. There experiential change occurs. The person may literally have a vision or auditory experience, which may take the form of a waking apparition or a dream, or the person's sense of life purpose may clarify and crystallise. Where a visionary experience occurs, it provides imagery and inspiration which is brought back into the person's life as part of their transformed identity. In the North American and other traditions this vision is often of an animal, a creature which becomes the person's spirit guide, or inspiration. Whatever the culmination, the intention is to discover a new relationship with life. This is a hope rather than a certainty, though, for the experience is invited but cannot be guaranteed.

Experiences of this kind rely upon achieving a particular state of consciousness. Changing consciousness is facilitated by changing the conditions which support ordinary life and the sense of self. Other conditions are often introduced which induce an altered state of mind: practices such as drumming and chanting, meditation and visualisations or even the use of hallucinogens. All of these will help to induce trance states.

Whilst such practices may seem exotic and far removed from ordinary life, in fact the experience of mild trance states is a normal part of the human mentality. We can all feel lifted by certain pieces of music or calmed by particular colours or environments. We are affected by dance and rhythms and moved by poetry. Harnessing such states for deeper spiritual and psychological transformation involves unhooking ourselves from the ordinary anchors of our identities and allowing ourselves to flow with the influences of conditions which will support positive changes.

Working in wild places for many people provides the discontinuity which is necessary to allow the mind to unhook from its habitual tracks and become open to such wholesome influences. It is also, itself, a source of new experiences and influences which can offer positive conditions for the emergence of new identities. Thus nature provides a place which both encourages the person to relinquish their old identities and also creates conditions for positive transformation.

Art can offer a form of transformational journey. The process of writing for example often involves entering a mild trance. When I am writing a book I find that I need to enter into a different mind-state in order to access my creativity. Doing this is not, however, straightforward. If I sit myself at my computer and will myself to write, the results are often turgid and slow to come. Pages written in this mode need a lot of editing to come into a form which flows for the reader. On the other hand, if I am in the right state of mind, the text comes as fast as I can type and hardly needs any correction at all when I reread it later.

This latter state is not necessarily something which I can enter at will. It seems to arise out of certain conditions. Sometimes I can create these circumstances, but even knowing what they are does not guarantee that a book will come together. More often it is a matter of getting on with life and not trying to write until, one day, I am surprised by inspiration.

There are some things which seem to help. In order to enter the state where the 'muse' takes over, I seem to need to create a space in my life that honours the process. This does not necessarily mean that I need to be rested. Sometimes when I write, I work very long hours. It does, however, need me to have enough mind space to prioritise the work. More than this though, the muse requires me to enter fully into the scene which I am writing about, particularly if I am writing a descriptive section or piece of fiction, but at other times too; allowing the visceral sense to become paramount opens the mind up to inspiration. I then feel and see and smell and imaginatively walk about in the space which I am writing about. I need to be there.

Once in the flow of a piece of work, I become completely absorbed, reluctant to let go of the keyboard and unaware of my surroundings. I can forget time, not hear conversations, and miss meals, all signs of an entranced state of mind. I am inhabiting the world of my characters or my narrative and have left temporarily the mundane world of the office. In this state, the words fall naturally on to my keyboard. If I do not feel this, I might as well stop and do something else and wait for the muse to return.

So, writing, like many other creative processes, is not a straightforward intentional activity. Rather, like a shaman, the writer enters a different space and there allows body and mind to be taken over by the spirits and inspired. Experience is mediated and transmitted to others through the process of writing, but once a book is written, it often seems to the writer that the tale has a life of its own. It is not mine, but rather has arrived as if channelled from some other shore.

Shamanic practices are often considered liminal. Liminal spaces are the border areas in which the norms of everyday life are suspended. Entering this territory take us across a threshold. We leave the structures which support our ordinary practical, psychological and spiritual make-up, and let go of aspects of normal reality. We discover a space where things become more fluid and where the boundaries of awareness shift from perception of the ordinary and take on different perspectives. Sometimes solitary, sometimes group experiences, we are carried by the process as much as we initiate it. We experience things for which we do not necessary have conceptions.

In our work with the environment, our initial grounding exercises and our silent walk around the site create a degree of trance. Participating in these lightly ritualised activities we attune our minds and bodies to a different way of being. We shift our focus away from the daily circuit of activity and slow our perception down, bringing our attention to the immediate, the growing, and the sensate. We notice that in doing this our experience changes. We become free to gaze or to wander amid the plants and trees and insects, the air, the sky and the earth. This slightly altered perception transfers into our work. It is a delicate, fragile flower, easily broken by carelessness. A chatty exchange, a hurried movement, a bungled instruction can all break the spell and bring the group back out of the trance to ordinary exchanges.

Sometimes, however, we work more deliberately with the idea of shamanic journey. On the first afternoon of the programme, Sundari and I suggest to the group that they explore the space of the site on their own, allowing the natural environment to speak to them. We are in the bonfire circle when we start. There are paths in many directions. We invite participants to choose a path and follow it, noticing as they go how the environment acts upon them at a body level. They will have two hours of solitude, long enough to become immersed in the experience.

We suggest that, as they walk, participants look for a particular place in which they feel drawn to spend time. They are to choose somewhere that seems to speak to them. Once there, we invite them to explore the experience of being, maybe through walking or maybe through sitting, to give themselves over to the experience of inhabiting the environment, and particularly to observe how their attention is drawn by objects within it.

In this state of openness, they are to ask themselves, "What questions does this space have for me?"

We focus on finding questions, not answers. Looking for answers leads the mind to search, to crave, to cling, but questions arise more spontaneously. We can hold them lightly as the week progresses, allowing them to drift through the back regions of the mind, like sand in an oyster shell, collecting accretions of wisdom as the tides of imagery and feeling wash over them. Later in the week, people will go back into their spaces and once again ask, "What is my question now? What is this space now asking?"

And so it evolves. We never formally ask for a response. If the space and the activities give one, that is good; if not, probably we do not need it. The whole process takes place in that in-between space. It is not discussed, but, rather, it filters between the lines of our being in the soft focused attention of the working trance.

A month or so after the exercise, I re-contact some of the people who participated, asking them if they would be willing to write about their experience. I am interested to know what it was like to participate, and also what stands out for them after this passage of time. Here are a few of the responses which I received:

Caroline: I set off from the circle around the fire and I think I already know where I am heading. I'm also aware of the places I avoid – the darker, cooler places in the forested areas - and instead find my way to one of the large uncut fields, full of wildflowers. I can stretch out here and I like the warmth of the sun. I settle down on the ground, the stems of the flowers surrounding me so tall that I disappear into the forest of stems. I get more intimate with what is nearby but still enjoy the expanse of the sky above.

After a while I ask, "Is there a question here?" and tune in to what I am noticing. I trace my finger along an area of soft green moss just in front of me. I watch a ladybird slowly making its way up the inside of a stem of cow parsley. "Do you have a question for me?" I ask the ladybird. It remains quiet. So I just settle into the warmth of the sun and bask for a while. I even take my top off so my skin can soak up some of the lovely rays.

Then I have a visitor. A beautiful butterfly! It lands right on my knee. I feel so honoured at this guest landing on my knee. I savour it; its colour, its gentle motion of wings opening and closing. I enjoy this encounter so much. For a while that is all there is! It stays for 5 minutes! Longer! Now there arises a dilemma. I need to move. I have been sitting cross-legged for quite some time now and my hips are starting to hurt. Also the weather has suddenly changed and the comfortable warming sun has now disappeared behind a thick cloud that has blown in and it's starting to rain. But oh, this butterfly is still here and I don't want it to go, it is just so beautiful. If I move it will fly away. In this encounter a question emerges... a bit unformed but something about how much discomfort/suffering am I prepared to endure in my attempt to hold on to something wonderful. Hmmm, interesting thought! And this is my question I take with me through the rest of the week.

Eventually I have to move – my legs are numb and I put my top back on feeling chilled! I let the butterfly go, thankful for its visit and a bit sad I have to truncate the encounter. But then something unexpected happens – the butterfly returns! This time it sits right on my nose! Incredible! I sit still again and it settles there, another 5 minutes! It feels like a lesson here! Ideas about letting go and of things returning drift in my mind. And again I enjoy this intimate meeting. Eventually it flies away and after what has been maybe 90 minutes I weave my way back to the campfire circle to reunite with the group, my question tucked under my arm.

Elise: *After lunch we meet at the 'bonfire space', [a] cleared area where stones have been placed to contain a fire, surrounded by benches. We're asked to go away on our own and find a space that invites us, and then to 'let a question form in the space'.*

In the feedback later, it emerged that for some people, the question was already there as they set off to find their space, and also that some people knew immediately where the space would be. Neither of these is true for me as I begin the exploration; as I set off I'm open to the idea that the space would invite me. I do have a strong sense of wanting to be in the open, not amongst trees; there is something around for me about wanting a clear view. After wandering along paths for some time, I see an opening in a hedge and make my way through into a large un-mown field full of white flowers bending in the breeze, with an open view of the countryside beyond. There's a narrow path leading along the edge of the field which I follow for a few yards; a small hollow in the hedge looks cosy and inviting, and I put my coat down and settle into the space. Ironically, given my desire for open-ness, my whole body is now below the tops of the flowers, and all I can see are the flowers and the sky. There's a sense of being in a secret and safe place. Until I look along the path and see the clear evidence of a probably quite large animal having been here quite recently. There's a slight tinge of anxiety – am I in something else's place? But I feel I've somehow committed myself to staying, so I stay.

My question starts to form, around the theme of place and whether this is where I want to be. How do I know if this is the right place? How 'right' does it need to be? There are butterflies and spiders about their business in the flowers; there's something grounding about the fact that they are just doing what they need to do without asking all these questions! I watch them and let my mind settle into stillness. As I sit, the weather starts to change; a wind gets up and it starts to rain. I put my coat on and settle back into the hedge, although I'm aware of a strong urge to get up and leave. My question evolves. How often do I stay somewhere (or with something) just because it's comfortable? How often do I leave somewhere (or something) just because it's no longer comfortable? What is it that makes me move away from experiences, to avoid them? I feel no need to answer; I'm not even sure if the question is fully formed yet, but it's growing, it's in process. By the end of the week it has given me guidance about what I need to attend to and explore further.

Writing about this some time later, I'm struck by how much of this process has made its way into my personal therapy; what I'm working with is indeed what the question pointed to, but this hasn't been a conscious decision and it's only now on reflection that I see the connection. Interesting!

Reading these two accounts, I am struck by the similarities: staying or leaving, comfort and discomfort, even a choice of open field rather than woodland. Maybe influenced by group process or by some collective unconscious preoccupation, for these themes had no obvious precursors in the group. A third account seemed to continue the theme of letting go.

Fiona: *We were asked to let a question come to us. It was at the beginning of our week of eco-therapy in the heart of France. We were asked to go out alone into nature, and to let a question arrive. Something that related to our lives at the moment. Something important.*

I left my friends and drifted, as I often do, towards the edges. The question came to me quickly, before I'd even found my spot – a hidey-hole under a bush. 'Can I let go?' I sat under the bush, with my question.

Our questions accompanied us for a few days. We were asked to live with them, like a koan. And then a few days later, we were asked to go alone into the woods or the fields and to let the landscape speak to us, to give us an answer.

Again, I wandered away from my friends, and was drawn to a hawthorn tree. One sprig held a perfect cluster of berries. A few at the tip were completely ripe – a deep red, delicious. Underneath, some of the berries were still green, tinged with a pink blush.

It occurred to me that the berries couldn't control when they ripened. They could do what they could – absorb the water from below and the sun from above – but the berries would ripen in their own sweet time. I had my answer. Trust. Let go. There are things I can do, and I should do these things, but so much of my life is beyond my control. My berries will also ripen in their own time. I just need to have faith. Trust. Let go.

Chapter Seventeen

Gratitude and Appreciation

It is Bio-dance week. Our eco-therapy group was last week. Now Massimo is leading a new group of people, and I am participating. He offers us an exercise which he calls *walking with gratitude*. During this exercise we will walk with a partner; one leading, the other being led. We are going to walk out from our home base in the bottom of *Champ de la Dispute* into the woods and fields around it.

As we prepare to walk, Massimo instructs us. The one being led should give him or herself over completely to the surroundings. Give attention to whatever arrives, whatever draws your eye. Hold it in your regard. Each time your eye is caught by something, repeat the phrase "I am grateful for... " And as you walk towards it, name whatever it is you are seeing. As you name it, look deeply at it; give it your full appreciation.

The group divides into pairs. I am partnered by a Spanish man who does not speak English. Our only language of communication is French, which neither of us speaks terribly well. It does not seem to matter though, for this exercise does not require understanding. The partner's role is as guide and witness, and witnessing can take many forms.

We set out walking up the hill. I am being led. I look at the field and the path ahead of me which climbs through the rough grass, a thin parting in the vegetation. It leads up the slope into the wood. A little uncertainly I begin the repetitions.

"I am grateful for the grass; I am grateful for the ground I am walking on; I am grateful for the grasshopper."

I smile to myself as the small insect jumps across my path and carries on its way, into the field beside me.

"I am grateful for the trees," I continue. I look at the saplings growing up among grasses and thistles of the meadow. They are indeed becoming trees, perhaps eight feet tall now. "I am grateful for the new trees growing taller... "

My companion is not understanding me. He is leading me on up the hill, but my words mean nothing to him. I appreciate his presence, quiet and companionable.

"J'ai la gratitude pour les papillons; pour les feuilles; pour les fourmis," I continue. I want to include him, to share my delight in all that lives around me. The French adds a poetry to my responses. Somehow it expresses my pleasure and appreciation more than English could. Voicing the experience of nature in any language is challenging. In some ways the limitations of a foreign vocabulary simplifies matters. But also, my struggle to capture elusive thoughts and feelings emphasises the limitations of any language in expressing our awe at the complexity and abundance of life. In the effort to voice my experience in a new tongue, it is as if I am struggling to communicate with the natural world itself.

We ascend the hill, winding through the new wood of young oaks and field-maples, passing a couple of crab apples, the fruits of which already ripening, and a hawthorn with red berries. Here we pass through a small clearing, scattered with mauve scabious and some white umbellifores, wild carrot I believe. There is bright yellow hawkweed and feathered grasses. I feel deep appreciation of the colours, the freshness, the prettiness of these flowers. It is the quintessential summer meadow in miniature. The morning has been grey, but now the sun is bursting through. Patches of blue are appearing between the clouds and the air is becoming warm.

Crossing into the wood we are soon beneath a canopy of mature trees. The path ahead is clear, edged with moss covered stones. To one side are the crumbling remains of a fallen trunk, which is also half encased in moss, fresh and green from the recent rain. I reach out and touch it as we pass, feeling its texture, soft and springy. "I am grateful for the soft, springy moss."

After twenty minutes we exchange roles.

We have reached the top of the hill and are standing at the fork in the path. One way goes back down through the field towards the place where we started, the other onwards, through the rest of the wood to meet up with the long-distance footpath which crosses our land. Known as the medieval road because of its unknown, but early, origins, it is cut each year by the local commune, the equivalent of an English parish council, it is wide and easy to walk. It forms a landmark and a point of easy access to the further parts of our site.

Now leading my partner, I decide to take the road through the woods, taking a longer route back to our starting point. I want him to have the opportunity to experience a variety of terrain. We take a moment to reconnect in the new configuration, standing together at the fork in the road, then we start to walk towards the medieval road. We cut through a gap in an old stone wall between two trees and turn onto the wide, grassy expanse of the track.

My partner speaks in his own language following Massimo's instruction to us, so I do not understand what he is saying, but it does not matter. I know that he is finding his own words to express the formula and is also putting his gratitude into language. As I witness his words, my heart understands the sincerity of his connection to the trees and flowers and insects.

Gradually in accompanying him and listening, though, I start to recognise some of the words he is using. Although I do not speak Spanish, many words are similar enough to other European languages for me to guess their meaning. Our common gaze at things we pass, spiders spinning webs, flowers in mauve, white and yellow, sunlight filtering onto the path all give me clues. I do not need interpretation. We share the delight and gratitude which wells up from the practice.

The track curves down between hazel hedges. Clouds of brown butterflies fly up from the flowers that grow low on the ground in the grassy central ridge between the tractor tyre marks left by the grass cutter. A buzzard mews from somewhere over the fields, out of sight. Then, finding our way back into the wood that curves around the lower edge of our land, we take a narrow path along the drainage ditch which runs back along the margin of the field.

It is not far to our home base. Others are already returning to the field, sitting together, talking quietly or meditating in silence. We join them. The whole walk has taken about an hour. We smile as we share our reflections. Different experiences, different interests, different paces and styles of doing the exercise, but so many moving accounts of special moments, of times when our appreciation became real and vibrant, when tears flowed and we felt joy.

It is later in the summer and I am running a day workshop in the Netherlands for women on the theme of guilt and judgement. In the morning we have spent time sharing personal experiences and feelings in the group circle and in pairs. We have done some grounding work and explored the ways in which we respond at a bodily level to situations in which we are afraid of being judged by others.

During our lunch break I reflect on the things which have been shared. How easy it is to get caught up in a cycle of guilt feelings, preoccupied with fears of criticism or recrimination, of having failed to live up to our view of how we should be, or the images which we see all around us. Mothering seems to be a particularly powerful area for generating feelings of guilt. There are so many ideals around in the media and amongst social circles about how mothers should be, and so much written in popular and mainstream psychology that points to the damaging effects of mothers on their children. Children are quick to capitalise on vulnerabilities, and for single parents maintaining a lone voice of discipline whilst providing enough love for two parents often leaves feelings of failure. I wonder how we can move out of this cycle of self-criticism and despair.

So it is that in the afternoon I suggest that we go out into the area of green parkland adjacent to the building where we are working to explore and to share some group exercises. It is an area of open land, with many trees and grassy stretches, steams and ponds. Like much of The Hague, you are never far from water.

Just as in France, we begin our walk in the room where we have been working by doing a grounding exercise. This both establishes a calm, body-centred mood and introduces a serious, silent atmosphere. We then walk out of the building at a slow, but not abnormal walking pace. We are in the area where most of the women live and I do not want to cause them embarrassment by asking them to act too strangely. Nevertheless we must look a little odd, walking in line in silence.

I am at the front of the line, and as we walk out I am immediately struck by the vibrancy of the natural world. A large clump of nettles grows by the side of the path and the leaves are vivid, stunning to look at in their green lushness. I feel that I have never seen stinging nettles so beautiful. Perhaps it is the morning's rain which has refreshed them, but maybe too our morning's exercises in awareness have opened my eyes a little wider.

Finding a quiet corner of the park, enclosed on three sides by rows of bushes so relatively private, we form a circle holding hands. We breathe in the fresh air and look up into the tall branches of surrounding trees which toss in the wind, for the week has been stormy and the wind has still not subsided.

Shutting our eyes we listen, hearing the sounds of the city. I invite the women to listen to it as if they are listening to an orchestra. The music of the city is surrounding us, I suggest, we can listen with appreciation to the bass drone of traffic, the staccato tones of children's voices, the counterpoint harmonies of rooks and magpies. We can hear the haunting refrains of geese. We stand, breathing the clear, rain washed air and listening.

I explain what we are going to do. We will use Massimo's *walking with gratitude* exercise. I ask the women to find partners. They pair up, then I give the instructions. Soon they are walking around the paths, one person from each partnership talking, the other silently witnessing. As they walk, with each sight they encounter, the woman who is speaking expresses her appreciation, holding the object which has caught her attention in sight whilst doing so. "I am grateful for... I am grateful for... "

After the exercise we come back together in silence and walk back to the meeting room. On the way, I suggest that as we walk, the women observe shades of light and dark, sunshine and shadow, as they play out in the trees and plants and structures which we pass. These bright and dark spaces seem to reflect the mental processes which we have been talking about. In the natural environment the light and shade lie side by side, complementing one another in a way that creates intricacy and attractiveness. But these latter thoughts are interpretations. I do not need to say actually these things. I leave the themes of dark and light to emerge later in our sharing.

Back in the sharing circle, the women talk about their experiences. Faces are bright and energetic. In some ways there seems nothing to say. A couple voice this. But others are keen to share. The feelings of guilt have dissipated. The quagmire of circling thoughts, "I am not good enough, they are judging me," have silenced. Deep peacefulness and contentment has replaced them. The radiance of the world is reflected in the women's faces. Outside the rain has started again. Our time breathing the fresh air and enjoying the sunshine feels like a special gift. The world is indeed beautiful and we are recipients of it.

The pull-along barrow is completely full of courgettes. This time of year the garden becomes so productive it is almost overwhelming. What do you do with a whole cartload of courgettes? After all the effort of digging and nurturing and watering, how could we let them go to waste, and yet our ingenuity is being sorely stretched. There are beans too. The climbing beans are covered in beautiful green dangling runners and the small bushy French beans are doing well too. Lettuces are now big green rosettes and the tomatoes are covered in ripening fruit. There are pumpkins chasing along behind the leeks, not yet in excess, but a few weeks will see us searching the web for pumpkin recipes.

We laugh at the excesses sometimes. Earlier this summer I managed to create a four-course meal entirely of courgettes, partly as a joke, but partly because I love the challenge. We had courgette and mint soup followed by stir-fried courgettes and other vegetables, a courgette and tomato salad and finally a courgette and raisin crumb-topped pudding for dessert.

Today, however, there is no shortage of variety to work with. We have a wonderful selection of vegetables and as I am cooking, I prepare a combination of our own potatoes, carrots, two sorts of beans, courgettes, tomatoes and broccoli in a coconut curry with huge lettuce and tomato salads. We eat vegetables till we can eat no more, finishing off with blackberry and courgette crumble.

In our French centre we have developed a way of cooking which is in close harmony with the garden. As cook, one begins preparation for the meal by walking round the vegetable beds, checking out what is ready for picking. Of course, as we take turns to cook for several weeks at a time, this means getting to know the garden intimately. It means that we see the vegetables growing bigger, maybe pull up a few weeds in passing, take small carrots from the row early in the season to thin out the rest, and pick things in ways which do not damage the plants. Often we just take outer leaves from cabbages or lettuces rather than destroying the whole plant, leaving the rest to continue to grow for longer. If you cut a cabbage and leave the root and stalk in the ground it will grow new small heads out of the side buds on the stem. One year we arrived at the centre in winter to find our cabbages had been frozen in the snow and reduced to a mushy pulp. We left them in the ground and went back to England, thinking we would clear them out in the spring. Several months later we were surprised to return and find that the plants now each had four miniature cabbages growing on its original stalk.

Sometimes, early in the season, there is not much growing. We then use wild food such as nettle tops, fat hen, or pig weed. Later as the garden reaches its peak we may be struggling to make sure nothing is wasted. At this point it is often a matter of thinking about what will keep another day or two and what will deteriorate if not used. Of course, we also make copious quantities of chutney and jam. But in autumn, we still enjoy finding wild food to add to what we grow. Living close to the earth helps us to engage in and appreciate its rhythms. Collecting wild food such as nuts, blackberries or fungi brings a particular feeling of symbiosis. To be fed by the natural environment is a special gift.

Since we approach the kitchen through a relationship with the garden, we rarely use recipe books to plan our meals. It is true that they can be useful sources of ideas, particularly where there is a glut of something, but more frequently we simply look at what we have got and ask it what it wants to be. With such fresh, organically grown vegetables, short cooking times and minimal spices often work best. Allowing oneself to be creative in the kitchen is very freeing. Many people are inhibited to experiment, but in fact with most vegetables one cannot go wrong, and many can even be eaten raw.

So cooking becomes a celebration rather than a chore, an

appreciation of the plentiful produce which the garden is bringing forth, and of the work of those who planted and tended the seedlings in their early days. With different community members moving between our different centres, often those who plant are not those who eat, so it is as well to remember those who dug the ground in spring when we enjoy its fruits in August or September.

The celebrative approach to food is supported by an attitude of appreciation and awareness in the cooking itself. I particularly like cooking for retreats since I like to make the preparation of the food into my meditation. Cutting up vegetables, one can consciously engage with the physical act, feeling the pressure as the knife splits the carrot or onion, and smelling the fresh scent of the vegetables and fruit. Working in silence, I relish the peaceful atmosphere of the kitchen, as I work steadily through the various tasks. Even though sometimes preparing a meal for a large group in a limited time can require a lot of concentration and involve complex tasks, dovetailing the preparation of different parts of the meal so that it is all ready for the planned mealtime, it is still possible to work quickly on a number of things simultaneously and also be at peace. Providing food for others is a great privilege and I am always humbled by how appreciative others are of the results. Shared meals are one of the nicest ways of giving and receiving kindness.

Other times, though, the kitchen is the social hub of the centre and it can be very enjoyable to share conversations over the cutting board. People often gravitate to the cooking as a place where they can both meet with others and also feel that they are contributing to community life. It is nice to be able to share some of the pleasure of our ways of working, which are often quite different from what people are used to in their own homes. Kitchens are traditionally associated with homely things, the place where we spent times with our mothers or with other kindly relatives as children, where we scraped leftover cake mix from big earthenware bowls or tasted newly baked buns, still hot from the oven.

When we are touched by those things which surround us and really see the riches of our environment, gratitude wells naturally up in us. It is innate response which burgeons when we stop our distractions and look at what we have. Yet our mentality is built on distractions and, in particular, we mostly operate from positions of self-entitlement which poison our minds against the wealth which life offers and the kindness and concern which other people show towards us. We misinterpret or think the worst too often. We tend towards criticalness or self-concern, or build our expectations and then become disappointed.

Too often we are counting scores and resisting imagined threats, fantasising that others judge us, or that their expectations are higher than they are. We fail to appreciate the ordinary because we have learned to overlook it and so miss out on simple joy.

The other-centred focus values gratitude. Encouraging appreciation, it draws our attention to those things which we otherwise tend to miss. It sometimes deliberately asks those questions[40] which will help us see how we have benefited from others, human and non-human.

In environmental work, however, there is often no need to deliberately invite reflection on these feelings. Exposure to nature brings so many special moments and unexpected treasures that we cannot but feel appreciation.

Chapter Eighteen

Acorns Among the Grass

We return to France in late September. The drive down is long and tiring, and having met a lot of traffic around Paris which meant a slow crawl through city traffic, we are relieved to hit the open road south through the lush forest of Fontainebleau and beyond. France has so much woodland. Royal hunting grounds apart, trees line the roads and grasp the hillsides, or cluster in little copses between the large open fields of agro-industrie. Even the motorway which we use is called L'autoroute de l'Arbre,[41] the motorway of the tree. It has tree themed picnic sites, and one of its service areas has an arboretum where one can take a stroll, taking a break from the motorway traffic for a while among the young trees which have been planted there. It seems strange to think of taking an outing to a motorway service area, but this one is visited by school parties, as the display boards there testify.

Our own region of Cher boasts a number of good sized forests. There are three within easy range of us and many others which are not much further off. They are mixed woodlands, deciduous for the most part, with chestnuts, beeches, maples and oaks. Tronçais, our nearest forest, can be seen stretching across the horizon to the south of us, as we stand on the ridge along the top of the *champ de la cave*, our biggest field. This forest is noted for being predominantly made up of oaks, and is well managed by foresters. Great lorry loads of trunks feed the sawmills along the way to St Amand Montrond, our nearest town. Good timber is always needed for building.

It is dark when we reach the house, after eleven o'clock at night. We see the old buildings in the headlights as we swing into the yard, familiar as old family members. The grass in front of the house is still neat and green, for we have only been away for a couple of weeks, and the rose bush in the middle of the flowerbed is covered in a fresh flurry of crimson flowers. The waxing moon which has been accompanying us along the way, promising us its fullness in the coming week, is veiled in dappled cirrus clouds. The air smells fresh with the night-time dew.

Suddenly out of the darkness there is a flapping of pale wings above the roof of the house. A bird lands on the chimney stack. It is a little owl. The creature perches on the brickwork, dipping down behind the chimney pot then peering out again, bright-eyed, its head cocked sideways, looking down at us with curiosity. It feels like a good omen for our return; a welcoming party. We have come home.

Late September often brings an Indian summer in our part of France, and this year it fulfils its promise. The days are hot, with the sun still intense at its zenith in a clear blue sky, although at night-time, as soon as the sunlight has faded, the temperature drops, and the early mornings have the sharpness of autumn about them, heavy dewed and chilly, yet bathed in the golden light of the late sunrise.

For the most part the trees are still green and the grass is growing in the cut areas of the field, but the elms in the hedge are turning golden yellow. We have work to do, harvesting the produce from the garden and turning some of it into chutneys and jams. Sometimes, though, we also just sit and enjoy the sunshine, relaxing in the warmth, appreciative of this extra time before the season fully changes.

The sun shines brightly for the first four days of our stay, but on the fifth day heavy grey clouds start to mass in the west. Storms are forecast, and, on cue, they arrive early evening. Thunder rumbles, at first distant, but later coming closer, reverberating against the stone walls of the buildings. The rain is falling. We sit in the attic of the house, once the granary, a boat-like room with big oak beams bowed over, supporting the wooden framework on which the tiles are laid. One can see their undersides, terracotta slabs, resting on cross struts. It is a simple construction. The rain falls on the tiles, drumming loudly. It is a comfortable noise, foreshadowing wintery evenings ahead, snuggled in blankets, chatting or reading.

By bedtime, the first storm has passed over, and the full moon is throwing shadows across the yard. I am sleeping in one of our outbuildings now, a cosy whitewashed cell, simple but timelessly attractive. The room is cosy despite being unheated, furnished with an old iron bedstead and small painted wooden cupboard. My nightlights sit, flickering gently in the lime-washed niches in the walls, throwing a warm light, too dim to read by, around the small sleeping space. When I extinguish them, the darkness is complete, velvet blackness. It is not much more indoors than camping. The air is fresh and cold, and I am far more aware of the change in the weather than the others who are in the house.

Throughout the night, waves of stormy wind and rain pass over and fresh bouts of thunder and lightning interrupt my slumbering. Sometimes the rain is heavy, its drumming insistent enough to wake me, but other times it fades to a soft fluttering, like fingers playing on the roof tiles, lulling me back to sleep. I feel content to flow with the changing sounds, drifting through the sea of showers, tossed in my dreams by the moving of the weather systems.

In the morning, when I finally awaken, the wind has dropped and the rain is coming down solidly. I open the door of my cell so that I can lie looking out, for, though I am not tempted to venture into it, the endless deluge of water which descends from the sky and the waterfall which is running off my roof into the gravelly hollow which it has worn outside my door is entrancing and soothing. I bed down under my covers, waiting for it to ease up, but at the same time enjoying watching its continuing force.

Eventually I have to accept that the rain has set in. A dash across the short distance to the house is enough to get me seriously wet, but I take it in good spirit. The shower is hot, and I have dry clothes to put on. By mid-morning, though, the rain has more or less stopped. It has indeed been heavy, for the various containers in the yard have three or four inches of water standing in them.

The storms have brought walnuts down from the trees. The tree in front of the house where we met in the summer has not produced much this year, but the one behind the house is prolific. Shirley, who has come with us for this autumn visit, and I take bowls to collect the fallen shells. Walnuts are ripe when the green husks split open. They scatter onto the ground as the wind shakes the tree. It takes a little time to train the eye to spot them among the rough grass, even though it has been cut relatively short, but they are easily felt under foot, hard round lumps that impress themselves upon the sole. Since the rain has also encouraged some new growth of nettles, collecting the nuts can be a painful experience and my hands are soon tingling with stings.

The nut collecting reminds me of childhood treasure hunts. My mother kept a jar of dry haricot beans which she used to bring out at parties and on days when we were bored. I don't believe she ever cooked dried beans, so the same ones must have lasted all our childhood. When we needed a diversion, she would scatter the beans around the house, hiding them in corners and throwing handfuls across the floor of the sitting room. We children would then be given paper bags and sent off to collect the beans up again. It occupied us for a long time, as did the meticulous counting which followed. I often think we had more fun with that jar of beans and a few paper bags than most children today have with their expensive shop bought toys, but perhaps I'm getting old. I notice, though, that I still have a competitive edge in my nut collecting. Even on my own, the karmic residues of those childhood games goad me to find every last nut among the rough grass roots.

A lot of walnuts are still on the tree. Some are unripe, but others hover in their broken casings, waiting for the swaying branches to shake them free. These can be picked directly. I collect as many as possible this way, since it is far easier and more comfortable than searching the nettles beneath. The husks stain my hands black so that I start to look like a weathered old woman of the earth. There are plenty of nuts and we have soon filled a couple of large plastic containers. I always feel great pleasure in harvesting such riches.

The weather is changing, and, with it, the winter season seems not so far away. The rain has chilled the air, bringing a new atmosphere to our centre. Walking round the site, the summer is already memories. Places which were important during our therapy week still hold their energies: the dance floor under the big oaks, the bonfire circle, the clearing with its wayward structure, the retreat hut, the secret field, the bamboo patch. Each is imbued still with many images of the group, of friends, of summer heat and the buzz of insects.

The paths are already growing brambles, so I carry secateurs as I walk. Squirrels are harvesting nuts from the hazels, stowing them away for the cold hard times ahead. They are bolder now, and we see their perky, rust coloured faces peering at us from amongst the branches, their tails flicking as they bound off into the arms of the trees. The mice too have already been cracking the nuts, and discarded shells litter the ground under the trees. The crab apples have fallen onto the ground and we pick them up to add to our chutney making, along with the continuing supply of courgettes and windfalls from the orchard. Susthama stirs the huge cooking pot, full of vegetables and vinegar almost continuously and the pile of filled jars grows in the kitchen.

The garden is at its most productive and the three of us eat like queens. We have so many vegetables now that we can hardly keep up. The freezer is overflowing and we still have more. Beetroots and carrots, broccoli and lettuces, beans and sweet corn, celeriac and cucumbers, leeks and tomatoes: the list is endless. The pumpkins sit like huge golden footballs amid their wilting leaves and courgettes the size of marrows turn up beneath their tangled parent plants.

We dig potatoes. How exciting, that first glimpse of clean, pale globes tumbling out of the turned loam. Once again, childhood memories surface. I recall how fascinated I was as a child by the tiny potatoes, miniature, doll's sized replicas of the full grown ones. Another treasure hunt, scrabbling in the earth to find them after my father had been digging, and then cooking them myself in the smallest saucepan my mother could provide. The land holds many memories.

This past year has been a time of transition for me. A difficult time, the ending of my marriage has taken me into a journey of uncertainty, but also of rediscovery. In this, the eco-therapy week marked a turning point. Whilst facilitating others in personal enquiries, I have myself discovered or rediscovered the new direction for which I have been searching. In some ways a new beginning, the process has been one of retrieval, soul retrieval perhaps, a journey back into my roots, our roots. A discovery of the treasure locked in my past, the past, but also here, now, breathing into my present.

Reconnecting with the earth has brought me back to what I have always known. It has given space for things which are most deeply spiritual to surface, and for the healing energy of the natural world to embrace me. As a child my refuge and my play was in the woods; days spent building camps and lighting fires, playing imaginative games and finding solitude among the wild spaces that hid themselves around my London home.[42] Now as an adult, those childhood worlds become the resource for my working life, as well as for my spirit. The wisdom that I learned from growing things, a heritage not expressible in words, comes into its own. Shaped by the years of working therapeutically and my spiritual practice, it creates the bedrock, which gives me new directions. As I walk across the land, recalling the summer activities, I feel a deep contentment, in love with the forests and the fields, knowing that wherever my future lies, this, the soil of places with which I feel such close connection, will be a refuge for me and something which I can pass on to others.

And so, as I go out into the woodland and the open spaces, I feel the coming together of many strands. Memories cluster, both general and specific. Childhood and summer mingle, their stories layering associations. The years spent here, the changing vegetation, the people who have come and gone, become part of my present as I walk the site. Last September I picked the walnuts with David. This year I am alone. I text him, and he replies, reminding me how he twisted his knee jumping off the ladder. I smile. We can still be good mates.

Perhaps the times are changing, or maybe not. The world is facing challenges on many fronts, and conflicting pressures drive its human population scurrying this way and that, searching for ways to guard its comforts. It is easy to become cynical or disheartened. As a teenager I was deeply worried by the threats which modern pollution caused to the environment. More recently, the complexity of green issues has become apparent, and, as factions debate solutions, commercial concerns have relentlessly overridden the policies of conscience. The confusion can be debilitating.

Solutions will need to come from big scale planning. It is easy to feel outfaced. Even the national frontiers cannot contain the threats of global catastrophe, so it is fitting that it is in that international, political arena that discussion takes place. But meantime, we also need to find our roots, to ground ourselves and reconnect. Only by doing this can we hope to heal our struggling planet.

So whilst this book has reflected on a very personal scale, exploring the different possibilities for environmental therapies and reflections, and looking through the lens of our individual encounters with the psychological and spiritual dimensions of working with the natural world, this grounding also provides a lens through which we can look out into the world and the universal arena. From the personal comes the collective. From the collective comes the universal. When we embrace the natural world we are changed. Through us, perhaps, the voice of nature, becoming our lover,[43] speaks out from the heart, and the powerful energy of living creation, the cycling of life and death and life, is unbound; released back into the world.

I thought for a long time about a title for this book. Nothing seemed quite right. All that came felt old and tired, corny or pedantic, uninspiring or overused. Eventually, I gave up struggling with words, stopped searching for the right answer. Instead I brought to mind the scene, last month, there in the dance space at the bottom of the meadow, where the spiders weave their webs among the long grasses of the field and ants scurry to and fro, carrying their burdens of straw stalks and butterfly wings. In my mind, I sat there once again, beneath the heavy boughs of the old oaks, in the shade of their green canopies. There beneath the trees were acorns; early fallen, and still emerald green, lying among the grass. I found my title.

The image speaks on many levels. At simplest it creates a picture: a summer afternoon in a field beneath the oak trees. It expresses the raw beauty of an encounter, a moment of seeing, caught in a single phrase. But more, it resonates with other meanings. Our fields are scattered with oak saplings. These trees, now hardly taller than a man, have grown to twice their previous height in the seventeen years since we first came here to our centre in France. Oaks grow slowly, and I will not live to see them reach maturity. They are our future and their lifespan rests in the hands of our children's children, just as the oaks which we sit beneath tell stories of peasant farmers, centuries ago. The trees are not planted. They have grown from acorns scattered by the wind and animals. All we can do is to stop ourselves from getting in their way.

Whether this book describes a therapy for humans or for the planet, whether it offers inspiration or methodologies, theories or stories, it speaks of possibilities, of ways of being which might provide conditions for a future. Perhaps it too is a scattering of acorns, thrown out by the wind into the long grass. Perhaps some of those acorns will grow.

Endnotes

1. This approach has been developed by those involved with the Amida training programme over the past fifteen years.
2. Brazier, C. 2009c, *Other-Centred Therapy*, O-Books.
3. According to a traditional story the Buddha was sheltered by a cobra whilst meditating during a storm soon after his enlightenment.
4. *Sabbasava Sutta*, Majjhima Nikaya 2.
5. *Alagaddupama Sutta*, Majjhima Nikaya 22.
6. The Parable of the Herbs in the *Lotus Sutra*.
7. *Vammika Sutta*, Majjhima Nikaya 23.
8. The vinaya, the behavioural code of the monks and nuns, specifically forbids unnecessarily destructive behaviour towards animals and vegetation.
9. *Bhayabherava Sutta*, Majjhima Nikaya 4; discussed in Chapter Twelve.
10. A more detailed explanation of this material can be found in Brazier, C. 2003, *Buddhist Psychology*, Constable Robinson.
11. This is explored further in Chapter Ten.
12. Brazier, C. 2009c, *Other-Centred Therapy*, O-Books.
13. A fuller exploration of the factors of conditioning can be found in Brazier, D. 1995, *Zen Therapy*, Constable Robinson.
14. There are many models of group process. The most commonly used one probably being that developed by Bruce Tuckman, and published in his article Tuckman, B. 1965, *Developmental sequence in small groups*, Psychological Bulletin, 63, 384-399.
15. Abraham Maslow developed the idea of the transpersonal as a counter to the preoccupation with the individual personal process in psychology.
16. Andy Goldsworthy is a sculptor in natural materials. His work can be seen photographically in a number of his books

including: Goldsworthy, A 1990, *A Collaboration with Nature*, Abrahams.

17. You can see some of Miya's work on his website at http://www.miyazakiwood.com/

18. Watson (trans), 1991, *Saigyo: Poems of a Mountain Home*, Columbia University Press.

19. Brazier, C. 2007, *The Other Buddhism*, O-Books.

20. A concept originally invented by the Austrian psychoanalyst, Wilhelm Reich and widely used by post-Reichian therapies.

21. The Satipatthana Sutta.

22. Majjhima Nikaya 10 and at Digha Nikaya 22.

23. Hymn: *Dear Lord and Father of Mankind* words: John Whittier, 1872. Music: Frederick Maker, 1887.

24. A therapeutic model using dramatic exploration which was developed by the psychologist Jacob Moreno.

25. *Lakshana* means a signpost or indicator. It points towards the self.

26. The third skandha, samjna, is concerned with association.

27. The 2008 film *Departures* (*Okuribito*) by Japanese director Yōjirō Takita.

28. *Samyutta Nikaya 35.*

29. Brazier, D. 1997, *The Feeling Buddha*, Constable Robinson.

30. Pali is one of the Indian languages in which Buddhist texts have been recorded, the other being Sanskrit. The collection of texts which are written in Pali are particularly associated with a school of Buddhism called Theravada, but they are recognized as foundational by most Buddhists. In Pali the word for a text is *sutta*. The Sanskrit equivalent is *sutra*. Thus, in referring to texts, since my own background is Pureland Buddhism, which relies more on the Sanskrit texts, I generally refer to texts as *sutras*, but in the case of specific texts from the Pali Canon, I use the term *sutta*.

31. *Majjhima Nikaya 4; translated by Thanissaro Bhikkhu as available*

on the website
http://www.accesstoinsight.org/tipitaka/mn/mn.004.than.html

32. Ibid

33. In fact at this stage in his life, it is incorrect to refer to 'the Buddha' and the Buddha is referred to as Gotama in the text. Gotama is the name of the man who became the Buddha. The term Buddha is an honorific title meaning Enlightened One, so is not used until after his enlightenment experience.

34. Ibid

35. It is also interesting to reflect on the relationship between primitive passions and the spiritual energy which is described in the *Ant Hill Sutta*, Majjhima Nikaya 23. I have discussed this sutta at length in my earlier book *Buddhist Psychology* (Constable Robinson, 2003).

36. *Mara*, the Buddha's tormentor, is literally 'deadness'.

37. Murcott, S. 1991. *The First Buddhist Women: Translations and commentary on the Therigata*, Parallax Press.

38. Dale Griffin speaking on the Radio Four programme *Saturday Live,* on Saturday 4th September 2010.

39. Stevenson, R.L. *A Child's Garden of Verses*, Puffin Books. (I was given this book when I was eight as a school prize *'for keenness in nature study and poetry'*.)

40. Naikan therapy is an other-centred approach which is based on questions. See: Krech, G. 2001, *Naikan: Gratitude, Grace, and the Japanese Art of Self-Reflection*, Stonebridge.

41. The A77, the first 'themed' motorway in France. http://lejardindessai.blogspot.com/2007/04/lautoroute-de-larbre.html

42. I drew on these experiences in my previous semi-fictional book, *Guilt*, O-Books 2009.

43. Macy, J. 1991, *World as Lover, World as Self*, Parallax Press.

Courses in Other-Centred Therapies and Eco-therapy are offered through Amida Trust. To find more information contact us on courses@amidatrust.com or write to

Amida Courses
The Buddhist House
12 Coventry Rd
Narborough
LE19 2GR
www.buddhistpsychology.info

BOOKS

O is a symbol of the world, of oneness and unity. In different cultures it also means the "eye," symbolizing knowledge and insight. We aim to publish books that are accessible, constructive and that challenge accepted opinion, both that of academia and the "moral majority."

Our books are available in all good English language bookstores worldwide. If you don't see the book on the shelves ask the bookstore to order it for you, quoting the ISBN number and title. Alternatively you can order online (all major online retail sites carry our titles) or contact the distributor in the relevant country, listed on the copyright page.

See our website www.o-books.net for a full list of over 500 titles, growing by 100 a year.

And tune in to myspiritradio.com for our book review radio show, hosted by June-Elleni Laine, where you can listen to the authors discussing their books.

mySpiritRadio